Brat:

Bentwaters and Woodbridge

1955-1959

Written by

James G. Byrd Sr.

"Mike"

Order this book online at www.trafford.com
or email orders@trafford.com

Most Trafford titles are also available at major online book retailers.

Printed in the United States of America.

ISBN: 978-1-4251-8721-7 (sc)

Trafford rev. 04/23/2012

Trafford PUBLISHING® www.trafford.com

North America & international
toll-free: 1 888 232 4444 (USA & Canada)
phone: 250 383 6864 ♦ fax: 250 383 6804

Special Thanks to These People:

Paul Byrd

For asking me to write this book.

Chris Byrd

For organizing the paper.

Vicki Prochaska

For typing the first copy.

Charissa Wiemann

For typing the book copy.

Julie Salisbury

For helping with the cover text.

Steven Hovel

For designing the book cover.

Mose Jackson

For being a friend since 1956.

And Lastly, Carol Byrd, my wife

For letting me use valuable family time to write this book.

INTRODUCTION

I was born in a little village in Easington, Yorkshire in England on March 26, 1946. My mom was a war bride from the east end of London. She was called a cockney. Dad was a farm boy from Wisconsin. He was on the B-17 and B-26 aircrafts during the war. He was one of the few that never got hurt but he did have to bail out of a B-17 on three different occasions. He was never interned in a POW camp. This book is about our four years in England during the 1950s. It includes what I did with my family, and how I had fun getting into trouble in sports and Boy Scouts. It wasn't until I was much older that I realized how much trouble I caused my dad with the authorities in the Air Force.

My brother, Paul, who is now a colonel in the Air Force, asked me to write a diary of the four years we spent in England. Being only six during the time we were there, he was too small to remember much. One thing led to another, and now it has become a book.

What I did caused my dad a lot of problems. No wonder whenever I got a spanking, Mom and Dad used my butt as a good target. I am ashamed of some of the things I did as I got older, like when Prince Charles and my brother got into a fight in the store on Thanksgiving

Day over a toy truck. I was going to hit the Prince in the nose but I stepped back because I did not want to get hit by my mom. She would have lit into Dad if he had not done anything to me. If I would have been better behaved, I feel Dad would have been a higher ranked sergeant in the Air Force. I never knew my dad had special skills in the Air force until he died and I talked to some of his Air Force co-workers.

I had a lot of freedom during our times in England which my sister, Veronica, hated. She always was mad at me because I had the run of the base while she was stuck at home helping Mom all the time.

I married a girl that I fell in love with my freshman year. I tried for four years to get a date with her but she wouldn't because she thought I was a cocky jock, which I was. Then, finally, with two weeks left of our senior year, she had enough and gave in. On our first date, I gave her my class ring, and then on our second date, I proposed to her. We have been married since June 11, 1966. We have two sons and between them, they have given us three grandchildren.

I would like to see some of my childhood friends that I mention in this book again. I would like to see Mose Jackson again who I found in 2003. We have gotten together once at our fathers' 79th and 81st squadron reunions. I would also like to find Betty Sue who is probably happily married with a dozen kids.

Well, read the book, have a laugh, and I hope you enjoy it.

April 26, 1955

"Iris! Iris! We are going to England! I'm getting stationed with the 79th at Woodbridge. We ship out in June!"

That was the beginning of four years that I will never forget. With these orders, my dad was given the opportunity for my mother to see her parents and seven brothers who she had not seen since May 1946 when my dad was stationed in Germany with the occupation force after World War II.

ONE

The trip from Laredo, Texas to New York was to be totally by train, but since there had been an avalanche on the railroad tracks in Mexico, our train could not get to Laredo. The train company put us on a Greyhound bus to San Antonio. We said goodbye to Joe and his family (Joe had married an English girl during the war and my parents had gotten to know them when we lived in Laredo for eighteen months). During our train ride we had to eat in the pullman cars. To us kids, it was real fancy, but to every day passengers it was nothing. There were a couple of things that stick out in my mind...I guess the biggest thing was the waiters. They were big African American men wearing really fancy clothes. Thirty-eight years later I found out that it was just their uniforms and they were required to wear them. They brought our food on these trays covered up with shining steel tops under which were dishes that were thick shiny white china. I don't remember much about the food, but I remember Mom telling us to eat everything because it was expensive. When I was older and my wife Carol and our boys traveled, I realized what Mom was talking about.

For entertainment, Paul and I would wander through the train. One evening we followed a man from the pullman through some sliding doors between the cars until he reached in his pocket and pulled out a key. He opened the door and went into the room that was making a deafening sound. Paul grabbed my hand and tried to pull me into the room. The guy turned around and told us that we had gone as far as we were going to go and that little boys were not allowed in the engine room. The sound and the smell were no match for anything we had ever been around.

The trip to San Antonio was about three hours, stopping in every little town on the bus route. We met a man that told us he was in England during the war and that he had always wanted to go back. He offered to change places with me and go instead of me, but I told him that I had been born in England and wanted to see my grandparents.

When we finally got to the train station, found our berth, and settled in, I remember Paul and I crawling up in our bed when the porter pulled them down to show us how they unfolded. We had traveled for two days in the train until we arrived in the big New York Grand Central Station. I remember stepping off the train and seeing all those big trains and the people running here and there to catch their trains (passageways) to all different points in the United States of America. After checking in with the station master, we were told there was a Navy bus on the street waiting to take all of the military personal and their dependents to the holding area. We waited at Fort Hamilton in Brooklyn in this holding area until our ship was ready in the Brooklyn Navy yard. Mom and Dad took us kids to downtown New York in a yellow cab. The Navy used to take the nice shining ships and run them into the depths of the sea and bring them back to the harbors, rebuild them and then send them out full of passengers. Now I know how the passengers on the Titanic felt as they were shipping out. The cabby took us to Fifth Avenue and while we were in his cab, he pointed out the Empire State Building, Time Square, and Joe Louis' Restaurant. Years later Dad told us that Joe had invited him to his restaurant for lunch. I guess Dad made quite an impression when he had met Joe during the war.

After supper on the evening before we were to board our ship, we walked along the harbor eating Cadbury candy bars. Mom told us that the following week we would get fresh ones in England. The wind was blowing in towards us and we were getting wet from the waves. That was my first taste of salt water, but being it was out of the New York harbor, it was probably more than just salt. Also during this last evening at the deporting barracks, we walked around the base. One thing I noticed was that the barracks were all the same and facing the same direction on the block. They were full of people that were waiting to ship out.

June 11, 1955

The next morning it was a little misty as we got on the buses to go to the ship. I remember walking up the gang plank and seeing everyone saluting everyone. We put our bags in the room that we had been assigned. Dad and I were to share a room with another man, while Mom was to share a room with Paul and my sister Veronica.

When the ship was pulling out of the harbor, there was a Navy band playing all kinds of military songs for us. We were all standing on the decks waving to the people on the dock and throwing streamers down. Then, I did not understand why we were doing this, but now I know that it was a Navy tradition for sending off all their ships.

Our ship was a converted pre-World War II aircraft carrier. It was called the USS Randall. I did not know that it was an old aircraft carrier until one day in 1984, a trucker came in to where I worked and saw my dad's old photo album. One thing led to another and soon he was telling me that he had been stationed on the Randall when it had been changed from an aircraft carrier to troop transport.

As our two little tugs pushed us out away from the dock, we began our trip out of the harbor. As we made a turn down the harbor, someone announced over the paging system that if we would like to look to our right, we would see the Statue of Liberty. I did not know what the Statue of Liberty really was until fourth grade Social Studies class. Years later my father-in-law and I actually had an argument about the Statue of Liberty (and of course I was wrong because he had a completely different view). Well, we got out of the harbor and the tugs left us. The captain pointed the ship out towards the North Atlantic and a six day trip to South Hampton, England.

TWO

In June, the North Atlantic is cold and choppy. It rains thirteen out of twenty four hours.

During our crossing, the first day was smooth. We had to have a lifeboat drill right away. From our room (which was two flights of steps below the top dock) we had to run up with our life jackets on to the Lifeboat Station 8A. The life jackets were so heavy (at least for an 85 pound nine year old who stood there wondering why in the hell we were standing there doing this when we could be having some fun). Standing there we watched the sailors going through the pretend ritual of sending life boats down the side of the ship into the water. In our group was a pretty little girl standing next to me. I remember she was blond and standing next to her sister and father (who was an officer in one of the other services). To this day I think her father was in the Navy. I remember looking at her and falling in love with her right away. Before the day was over, I was walking the deck holding hands with her, which we did for the rest of the trip. We were together most of the time when we were not sleeping. Most of the time we were on our own, but once in a while her little sister would tag along.

The first meal we had on our ship was something that I will never forget. It was my first taste of boiled cabbage. The Navy took big heads of cabbage, cut them in fourths, and cooked them (the only other time I had boiled cabbage was at the Great Lakes Navel training base for an Explore Convention in 1963). As we were passing through the dining area my dad told me to take only what I was going to eat because sailor cooks become unhappy if you don't eat everything. I can still smell that kitchen to this day.

As we sat down to eat I noticed there were waiters running around with white starch jackets, pouring coffee and helping the families with little children. The big white plates they served were a first for us. These plates were like platters to us kids.

After we ate supper and returned to our sleeping quarters, they made an announcement over the paging system that there would be a movie shown in the upper deck. I asked Dad if we could go. He said "sure," and I remember walking in with my dad and with my new ship girlfriend. During the show (of which I don't remember) I kept thinking "Why does my dad have to be here? I can't do anything!" Twenty-five years later and with two boys of my own, I know now why Dad kept a close eye on me.

Day two started with some sailor blowing his whistle in the paging system telling us it was first call for breakfast. I remember thinking, "who is this fool telling us to get out of bed and eat?" Mom usually told us to do that, and with a little less whistle. We got dressed and ran up two flights of stairs and out the door towards the dining room. When we got to the door, something hit us in the face. It was the spray of the sea. There was a sailor standing guard making sure that we were holding on to a lifeline when on deck. Evidently, the sea had gotten sick during the night and was trying to make us sick, too.

It was a traditional Navy breakfast. Eggs, bacon, toast and some real bad looking stuff they called "hash." After breakfast everybody was free to go. I remember two other boys, my ship girlfriend, and I checked out a game of Monopoly. The sailor we checked it out from told us that if we lost anything we would have to pay for it. So what happens? I shook the dice and the ship swayed, and I lost a dice. I told the sailor in charge that we needed another dice. His response was the typical military response- "Turn in the old one and you'll get a new one." So, back to the table and under the heating system I went to try and retrieve the dice. I was lying on the floor with my hand under the big metal frame when someone behind me asked, "What in the hell are you doing?!" I jumped, almost cutting my arm. I stood there looking at a big, heavy, mean-looking sailor and saying "trying to get my dice back, sir, so we can keep playing the game." He told me to forget it and to turn in the game and get back to our parents. Instead we walked the halls of the lower deck which is called the "whole of the ship." Soon the two other boys decided to get back to their rooms with their parents. This left me and my sweetheart to roam on our own. We were walking past a room where I heard all kinds of noise when a sailor told us we were in a restricted area by one of the engine compartments. Before we left he had taken both of our names to tell our parents, but to this day I think it was just a scare tactic.

Lunch and supper went on as normal. After supper, we kids got together for another Gene Autry western and a Woody Wood Pecker comic. The movie turned out to be so rotten that the two boys that were with us decided to leave. My sweetheart and I moved to the back of the room. I thought it would be nice to hold her hand. Things were going O.K. until I felt a hand on top of mine which scared the heck out of me. Looking back to see whose big hand was crushing mine, I saw that my luck had run out and her dad had joined us and was extending his Navy smile saying "that's enough." Thirty years later I think he thought my hands were going to explore the world.

On day three, the waters were rougher than ever. Nobody was allowed on deck unless they had a life vest and held on to the lifeline. The highlight of the day was when I went to supper that night. Going through the supper line, I noticed some eggs sitting on top of this green stuff (later I found out it was spinach). I had just sat down next to Paul and Dad and taken a bite of this "stuff" when I began feeling sick. I took off in a dash towards our room. Opening the room, I threw up on my dad's summer dress khaki uniform. I had crawled up into bed and was lying in the bunk when my dad came in and saw what I had done. He asked why I couldn't have cleaned up my mess. I got sick again at the thought of it. This was the only time I spent the night in the bathroom throwing up from rough weather (in 1985 I was on the British Channel in gale 10 force laughing at my wife for being sick due to the rough water).

The next morning I woke up feeling fine and went to breakfast. The water was a little smoother. After breakfast we went walking around the ship. We had turned a corner and horror struck me. My ship sweetheart said the Marines looked busy. I remember saying our ship was leaking. There were two Marines sand bagging the whole side of the ship where the gang plank goes out. They told us to get out of their way. I knew then I was going up on deck. Since I didn't know how to swim, I wanted to be near the lifeboat just in case the ship had sprung a leak.

That night I spent some time at the show, walking the deck and wishing I could stay with this girl the rest of my life. During our evening, we managed to get in a few dark corners for a little kissy face. We kept saying when we got to our bases we would write each other and I was so stupid that I never did get her address, let alone give her the address of my relatives. I remember standing on the bow of the ship looking at the sea and pretending I was Marco Polo saying "One day, I will be a sailor and ride the high seas." That attitude changed in 1963 when I went to the Great Lakes Naval training for an Explore Convention station when I was in Boy Scouts. All the "B.S" that came along with the Navy made me say "not THIS kid."

The last morning on the ship had finally come. To me it was a very sad time. I had to say goodbye to my ship sweetheart. I did not get her address or find out where her dad was stationed, so to this day I don't know what happened to her.

When we docked at South Hampton on the 19th of June, I saw the ship Queen Mary across the channel where we were docking. When our tugs finally pushed us up to the dock and the ship was tied down, they decided to drop this ramp down where I was standing. So, I thought "well I can get off now." I walked down this wooden ramp to the bottom and I heard "Get back on that ship, young man! You can leave when your parents leave." So back up the ramp I went – always looking over my shoulder making sure that this big MP didn't come get me and through me in the water. Standing back on deck, I heard my dad call me to help carry my bag. They put us in long lines on the ship with all of our bags. We filed down the ramp that I had already made one trip down. Once we got off the ship we were put on big old English buses and taken to a military compound named Shaftesbury. We lived there for a few days until Dad received his final orders for Woodbridge. While we were at Shaftesbury, we spent our time getting used to land again and making sure our shots were up to date (Man! Did we ever get shots back in those days!).

When they finally let us out of the base, we went to a nearby town and got on an English coal burning train to London (this was my first encounter with an old steam train). We were off to visit our Grandpa Dawson!

THREE

Grandpa Dawson was still living in the house where my mom was born (in 1972 our son Jon was conceived in mom's old room during a return visit). Again, it was 1955. Grandpa was living in this house with my Uncle Percy. In the backyard, he still had a bomb shelter. Mom showed it to us and described how she would sit in it for hours and knit while the Germans tried to destroy England with bombs. Grandpa's house was built in early 1900. It is a beautiful house that was home to my mom, her sister, and six of her seven brothers along with my mother's parents. My grandpa's house was right in line with the runway for Hinden airbase. It is now a British museum.

We stayed with Grandpa a few days then boarded a train at Liverpool Station for Woodbridge. In those days the trains moved slower and stopped in every little town. We were on a direct train to Ipwich, then changed to a train for Woodbridge.

When we arrived in Woodbridge, I remember getting off the train and walking up stairs that went over the train tracks. Just as we got over the top of the train, it let off a big puff of smoke. We were all covered in soot from head to toe. My mom laughed and told us that when she was a little girl she and her brothers (my uncles) used to stand on the crossing just to get in the smoke. (I guess it was a sort of ritual for all English kids).

After leaving the train station we walked up the little hill toward the town. Looking back, I could see the station was sitting on a river bank. It was the Deben River. The tide was out and you could see all the house boats stuck in the muck. Some were old PT boats, shore patrol, and just old-fashioned sailing boats. To this day, I can still see the women hanging out the wash on the mast poles and hear the tea kettles whistling on the stoves. Any how, we got up the hill, turned right, took about six steps and went into the Crown Hotel. This is where we stayed until my folks found a little cottage in Bromesville.

The first night at Crown Hotel was the first time in about one month that we had gotten to sleep in a real bed and had a soft pillow. There was Paul in the middle, Veronica on one side and me on the other side. Veronica did a good job of keeping all the blankets on her (even though it was June, it was still cold--waterbeds were something of the future).

The next morning, Dad went out to Woodbridge base and checked in. Before Dad went out to the base, my folks took us to some little restaurant for a breakfast that I will never forget. It was the best toast and jam I have ever eaten (except the one my wife makes from her fresh berries). We sat at a little table on the sidewalk that had an umbrella on it. While we ate we could see the train that we had gotten off the day before come into the station. Just before the train left, it let off a baller of black smoke. This time we laughed at the poor devils getting sprayed.

After breakfast we put Dad into the taxi cab for Woodbridge base. The cab drivers name was Cliff and he became a family friend for the next four years. Old Cliff took us to the town many times from the base to catch the train. Cliff, as all of us on the base used to call him, was a very good friend of Mr. Cooper (who was the old base commander of Woodbridge RAF base during World War II). Two years later I got to know Mr. Cooper very well because I was to work for him delivering milk, bread, eggs and the Stars and Stripes to the base housing. Cliff thought my little brother Paul was very neat with his tight curls. Cliff used to sit in his black cab and talk to us kids, telling us stories of all the different bombers that used to fly in and out of Woodbridge base.

Most of the first day was spent walking around town looking at all the neat shops. English bakeries usually had a special smell. No matter how full you were it always made you hungry. The butcher shops always managed to have a freshly killed chicken or two hanging from a pole in front of the store. The vegetable store had barrels of fresh brussels sprouts grown in the Midlands and little red or white potatoes grown on Guernsey Isle. Now the candy store, or sweet and tobacco shop as they were called, was a place every boy and girl should go. First, you would smell the pipe tobacco that the old Navy boy behind the counter was smoking. I remember buying my first ounce bag of jelly beans for three pence.

The main street of Woodbridge was one way. The big double-decker buses used to try to squeeze by where the cars were parked on the sidewalk. It was a thrill to ride on those buses. Every time they turned a corner, you could feel that big red machine sway.

There was an old co-op store on the main street. When you paid for your goodies they put the money in these cannon like cans and shot it up to some people sitting on the second story. These people recorded what you bought because this was a co-op where they paid dividends at the end of the year. A few doors down was the big Woolworth store that had everything from tea kettles to mouse traps. On market day they would draw all the farmers in from Ipswich to Loftous. By now, Dad got checked in to the 79th FBG as Assistant Hanger Chief working on the F84F.

FOUR

The next thing Dad did was to find us a house in a small village called Broomsville, about three and a half miles out of Woodbridge and about four and a half miles from Bentwaters' Air Force Base, where I would go to school for the next four years.

The house that we were to live in for the next four months was white with a thatched roof and no flushing toilet. We used to have to walk out around the house to another room where the toilet was. Under the peaks and overhanging on the roof there must have been one hundred mud houses that the swallows had made. I can remember going outside and ducking as those birds took dives at us. Mom used to chase those birds with her broom (thirty years later swallows built nests under our garage and Carol used to get mad at them, holler and chase them with the water hose. I would laugh at her until she would call me a S.O.B and spray me). About every two weeks, Dad used to take all our toilet waste and bury it in the backyard which had an orchard of apple and plum trees. The grass was always about two and a half feet tall and never got mowed. It was tough enough that even though you might want to mow it, it would have broken the mower.

Besides the grass being so tall, you were always falling into the hole from weeks before that you dug to bury the shit.

The house didn't have any central heat except for the fire places. All of the furniture was from the Queen Victoria era or older. Our neighbor lived in a big red house. She was an older woman who had to be in her seventies. Her son and his family also lived with her. I can remember her grandson. He was a few years older than me, but he used to take me around the area and show me where things were.

The village had its typical English country church. I think it was built back in the 1700s. The only time I was in that church was to take some fresh fruit there for Thanksgiving. The thing that sticks out in my mind about this village is that there were some brick steps going down from somebody's yard. My Grandpa Dawson came up from London one day and brought us two English bikes. The first time I got on it, I ran straight into the steps and flew over the handle bars and landed halfway up the staircase. As I was laying there in pain, Dad was yelling at me to get up and not be so careless. Old Grandpa Dawson was getting red in the face from laughing so hard at me.

Besides us, Bromesville had another American family in it. They lived next to the oldest man in the village. One day, the old boy was riding his bike home when he saw a F84 crash into the banks of the river Deben. He tried to get the pilot out of the plane, but it caught on fire and he had to leave him. That was after he had already burned both of his hands. When we kids went over to visit him that night after tea, his hands looked like he had boxing gloves on. He felt really bad that he could not get the pilot out. This crash was the first of three in the four years at Woodbridge.

Other then farmers living in and around the village, there was a cricket bat maker. He had been making them since before the war (when we went to England again in 1985, they were still making them only the yards were fuller with more finished bats than raw ones).

While we lived there I got to know this lady that had a big garden. Once a week she would have us young boys from the village work in her garden. She paid us two shillings and six pence and gave us some really good sweet cakes. Twenty years later I still remember how to plant leaks (an onion plant). There was another family that had a small greenhouse and grew vegetables for some of the local shops. We used to go down to their greenhouse and buy fresh tomatoes. One thing I remember about this family is their two daughters. One week during the summer of 1955, my uncle Graham came to visit us and with the both of us being adventurous and crazy, we got on my English bike with handlebar brakes and began to ride down the hill past the greenhouse. We began to go down rather fast (pick up speed) on this dirt road and I became scared. I grabbed the brakes which caused us to skid on the gravel. We flipped the bike over and the brake handle ran into my knee. My uncle Graham cut his arm and to this day we both have scars from this. Anyway, the two girls that lived in that house by the greenhouse were standing there laughing at us. Uncle Graham's quick Yorkshire response was "What the bloody hell are you laughing at? We both are hurt!" Uncle Graham picked up the bike and began to push it up the hill while helping me walk. When we got back to our house my mother quickly bandaged us up and gave us hell (or should I say she gave Graham hell for giving me a ride on the handlebars). Man! Did I hurt! The bar of the brake must have gone into my knee about one inch. For about one month, I hobbled around with a bandage on my knee with puss draining out of it. I remember Mom took me to the doctor in Woodbridge and he poured some stuff on it that almost put me on the moon. Well, my cut finally healed up and Graham went back up to Loftus and I kept riding my bike.

During that summer, I met a young guy that lived on a farm with his dad. That was my first exposure to a cow getting milked. I used to watch this kid sit on a wooden stool and milk these six brown and white cows, pour the milk in a big can, load them on a wagon, and take them down to the end of his driveway so a bigger milk truck could come pick them up. He would do this every morning.

Another thing that I thought was neat back in 1955 was how he would cut and harvest hay. He would have the two big work horses pull his hay cutter around the field. The next day, the same two horses would pull a rake around the hay and put it into rows which he would pick up with a pitch fork and throw into a big wagon. Instead of taking it to a barn like we do now, they put it into a big haystack out in the field near the barn. Farms in Bromesville had an average of 40-80 acres. Looking at it in those days, it looked like fun, but when I got older and began to throw bales of hay around on Walter Mielkes farm in Wisconsin, I found out how much work farming really was.

Near Bromesville there was the road that led to Bentwaters. On this road was a small garden shop that sold juice and fresh vegetables. When they were open on weekends, we used to walk to the roadside stand and buy some of the best lemonade I have ever tasted.

On Saturday mornings while we lived in Bromesville, Mom would go to Woodbridge and buy the fresh produce for the week. I remember one week Mom sent me to town to do the shopping. I had made up my mind that I was going to go to the show that afternoon. I went to all the stores Mom never went to because of the low grade of food even though it was at a lesser price. I had plenty of money left over so I went to the show. I was scared of missing the bus so I left halfway through the movie. On the way to the bus stop, I stopped at the sweet shop and bought Mom a box of candy. I wound up on the wrong bus and had to get off about four miles from Bromesville and walk home carrying a bag of half-spoiled fruits and vegetables.

When I finally got home, Mom could not believe that her regular stores would sell such bad food. I couldn't lie so I told her what I had done and gave her the box of candy. Since I had a job and Dad didn't get much money (especially for non-essentials), Mom told me I was going to have to pay for the candy.

School finally started. I was enrolled at Bentwaters' Dependent School. My fourth grade teacher was Mrs. Finley (a few years later her husband was lost in the Atlantic Ocean when his F86 went down).

We used to get on these big English buses out on the main road. The bus used to take about twenty minutes from Bromesville to school. Every bus had an air police assigned to it. They were a great bunch of guys. I've forgotten the name of the AP on our bus, but the most famous was a colored AP named Johnny Johnson who was assigned to the north bus route. Bentwaters' school in 1955 was made out of green Quonset huts. There were about three buildings put together for grades 1st through 7th. The playground was about 70 percent blacktop with slides and swings. We had a ball diamond and a field to play soccer or football. Another thing was that our playground was well equipped with bomb shelters. There were two of them left over from World War II. Right next to our school was the base mess hall. To the west of our playground was the NCO Club and right behind that was the base commissary and officer club. Halfway through my fourth grade year, the NCO club started serving hot lunches for us students. What sticks out in my mind about those meals were oyster crackers and this stew they called Mulligan Stew.

I joined the Cub Scouts that fall and I had a den mother who was living in the housing at Woodbridge (her husband was stationed there). I've forgotten her name but I remember her house. It was a converted red double-decker bus. Back then the housing on base was a lot of trailers, old shacks and anything else that people could make into a house.

On October 3, 1955, Dad got his new Ford Angler Saloon with a 1772 cc engine. It was a two door blue four-seater. We kept it until 1963 when Dad traded it for his 1957 Chevy. Dad had also ordered me a new three speed bike from the PX and we had to pick it up there. The trunk was pretty small on the car and I almost had to ride it home. Any how, we got Dad's new car and my new Churchill Deluxe bike home (in one piece). I look at it now and wonder how Dad could afford payments for a new car and buy me a bike. The sacrifices my folks had to make are unexplainable. This bike took me many miles around England and Wisconsin and now it hangs in my garage.

FIVE

We stayed in Bromesville until November when Mom and Dad found a house in Felixstowe. It had an indoor bathroom and it had three bedrooms so Paul and I got to sleep together. Veronica had a bedroom of her own, and Mom and Dad finally had a room to themselves. The only bad thing about living in Felixstowe was that our bus trip to school was over an hour.

Our house in Felixstowe had a fish pond in the yard. One day while waiting for the bus, I stepped through the thin ice and got my foot wet. Going to school on those old buses without heat was a real treat. Mom never did figure out why I got such a cold. The backyard had some gooseberry bushes in it and as they came into season we would eat them off the plants.

While we were off on our Thanksgiving vacation, Mom and Dad took us kids to London to shop in Harrod's store. We took a bus to London for the day and it picked us up out in front of our house. When we were in Harrod's, there were some bodyguards that came into the store to check it out and went outside. All of the sudden Mom said, "There's Prince Charles!" He was standing next to my brother Paul looking at some trucks. Prince Charles and Paul were fighting over the same truck but I was scared of getting beat by Mom for hitting Prince Charles. If I had hit him while the Queen and Prince Phillip looked on, Dad would have caught hell from Mom for not giving me a spanking right then and there. Well, the Prince got a truck while Paul and I continued to look on. The royal family was doing their Christmas shopping. Most people in the store didn't pay much attention to the royal family because back then the royal family would walk the streets to any place without any trouble. Years later Mom and Dad would talk about the Thanksgiving Day we spent with the royal family.

Our bus ride home that night from London was quite cold because most English buses did not have heat in them. The kid sitting next to me got off in Ipswich and I noticed that he was walking strange. Mom said that he had club feet and that was how I would have walked if I didn't have my operation.

I would gather up sticks and fallen branches and store them in our coal shed. This house had five fireplaces and a cook stove in the kitchen. When Mom started up the stove in the kitchen, all of us would get out of bed and run down to the kitchen to get dressed. The year and a half that we lived there, the only fireplace I saw lit was the one in the living room. I got the feeling that the ones in our bedroom were too dangerous.

Shortly after we moved in, a British Chanbery Bomber crashed between a big truck stop restaurant and an open field. On the other side there was a school full of kids. Fifty feet further either way could have been worse because the restaurant was full of people and the filling station was a big truck stop. The RAF had a big military funeral for the pilot at the base that we drove through every day for school. On this particular day, I had been a bad kid on the bus and I had to sit on the steps of the bus so I never got to see what was going on (Man, was I ever mad at our AP!).

This particular RAF base had been bombed during the war and one of its hangers was hit leaving only one wall. It looked neat to us kids, but some of the RAF boys had been killed in the bombing. The wall that was left was used as storage in 1955 (When I returned in 1985, the wall was still standing. I tried to get near it to get some pictures, but an English bobby told me that I'd better not because this base had been converted into a communications station for England).

During fourth grade several things happen that stick out in my memory. I guess the biggest is when we put one of the guys up to stealing things out of the school supply room of our school. We would tell him what we needed, give him some money, and he would get what we asked for. We had quite a supply until one day he got caught. I don't remember our principal that year, but man, did he get in trouble for it.

That fall we got used to rainy, foggy days. When it was too foggy, the buses wouldn't run and our base would close up and all planes were grounded. The AP would be on double duty and they would have to a watch all the planes and building extra close for terrorism.

At Christmas time, we had a typical Christmas celebration. My folks always gave us kids a big Christmas present, dinner and bonbons. We would pull the bonbons apart to get a hat from inside. As usual, we got a lot of presents. Mom would order most of them from the Sears catalog back in September because it would take two or three months to arrive from the States.

During Christmas vacation, I met an old man that worked at one of the nearby farms. Josh, as we called him, was a World War I veteran. He lived in a house that used to be a barrack for a gun emplacement. It was near the coast and harbor of Felixstowe. We used to sit in his living room and look out the window with his binoculars that he had saved from World War I toward Harwich. Between his house and the harbor there were pastures where Josh kept his cows.

There were still remains of the gun emplacement and these were not little guns. There were big cannons that probably could have shot halfway across the British Channel. Some of these guns were covered with grass and we kids used to climb up on top of them and look out over the harbor. Most of the time, it was a game called "King of the Mountain."

Josh was head herdsman on this farm, and during vacation I helped him. I never got any money, but the experiences were rewarding enough. For example, I would get up at 4:30 a.m. and ride my bike the two miles to the farm and walk out to the pasture with Josh to get the cows in for morning milking. My job was to feed the cows and calves while the three herdsmen did the milking. The calves were in pens by the big bull pens. To this day, I have never seen bulls as big as them. One day while I was feeding the calves, I thought my number was up. One of the old bulls had busted through his pen and was stopped because his body wouldn't go all the way through the hole. I was screaming so loudly that Josh and the Irishman came running to see what I had done. This was the beginning of my dislike for the Irishman. This tall red-haired man accused me of teasing the bull and getting him mad. From that day on I had problems with that guy. The Irishman (I have never been able to find his real name) lived in a red house on the road going to the farm. I tried my best to get even with him. One day, I threw fresh cow shit into his garden, but he caught me and made me fertilize his flower garden with it. My next plot was to destroy some of his flowers. This I did manage to pull off. I can still see those flower plants hanging over his brick fence. Those were the prettiest flowers I have ever seen hanging on a brick fence.

While I helped on the farm, I learned how to lead a bull from one barn to another. This farm had three bulls and every once in awhile they would move one of those big creatures to serve the cows. One other thing I learned was how to chase calves and throw them into a muddy pen. Once you fall down you learn how to stand up in the mud that has been coated with fresh runny manure. I fell once and decided that the next calf that got out was on its own!

SIX

Christmas vacation of 1955 ended and it was back to school for us kids. The first day was a new experience. When we got up, there was snow on the ground. We kids got dressed and hurried out to see what snow was like. After getting wet, we thought we better get back in the house because our 5'3" mother was yelling at us.

When we got on the bus, I went to sit in the seat that I had always sat in. I just about sat on a little girl that was in my seat. I told her to move over because she was in my seat. The little blonde smiled and moved over. I quickly told her that my name was "Mike" and that I was in fourth grade. In a southern accent, she said, "My name is Betty Sue Howel." This was the beginning of a three year friendship that I can still remember.

As luck had it, Betty was assigned to Mrs. Finley and she wound up sitting next to me in class. This was because I had introduced her to Mrs. Finley and explained that there was an empty desk next to me. For the next three years, Betty and I did just about everything together. Looking back at it all, I wish that I could have done more with her.

Every day while we would wait for the bus, an old Englishman would walk his dog in front of our house. The dog was a little black

Scottie. We became good friends but we never did find out this guy's name.

It was in March that my dad took his first leave so that we could go up and visit my grandma and uncles in Loftus. From Woodbridge, it was a long ride. In the train, I remember stopping in one town and my mom and dad woke us up and bought us some caramel candy. It tasted so bad that I have never eaten caramel candy since then. Anyhow, we arrived to Loftus. We had about a two mile walk from the train station to Grandma's house and the worst thing was it was all uphill (and I'm not just saying that either!) Grandma's house was in an old mining town and in her backyard was a shell tip. It was the slag that was left over from the ore that was mined in the ground underneath the village. Grandma Dawson lived in a house at the end of a long row of mining houses. My uncles, Robin, Graham, and Adrian, along with a step-grandpa Ralph and his son Ralph all lived with her. Young Ralph worked on one of the small farms nearby which had a little stream running through the farm and along one side of the creek there was an old stone wall that was built in the days of the Romans. We used to play Calvary over that fence and through the stream.

Grandpa Ralph worked for a company that hauled sand and gravel in big dump trucks. I remember once Graham and I rode with him on one of his routes and at lunch time he found out that Grandma had given him a plain cheese sandwich and was he ever mad when he got home. He told Grandma not to pack a lunch like that again (ten years later I told my wife the same thing because she had packed me a cheese sandwich on the first Friday that we were married).

During March in Yorkshire there are always baby lambs being born. In the Moors, the farmers raise sheep by the hundreds. Most of the farmers let their sheep run wild until it is shearing time. Watching the lambs run after their mothers was something that you never forget. All the sheep look the same and yet, the lambs still manage to find their right mother.

Up in northern England the terrain is very rough and rocky. The heather grows all over and in between what was the old Roman wall.

If you looked close enough on some of the cliffs overlooking the North Sea, you would see old pill boxes left over from World War II. There were a lot of them built in the north because the Germans would try to sneak in from the north and shoot up the coast harbors.

This being our first trip to Yorkshire, my mom and dad took us to the village where I was born. This village was also where my parents had gotten married. I was born in a two bedroom house. The houses were built around a square and the church was on the edge of the village. The water that was used to give me my first bath was drawn from a horse trough.

During this visit I also got to meet Mrs. Dowson. She along with Nurse Lindley helped deliver me in 1946. I continued to communicate with Nurse Lindley until 1972. In that year, I put flowers on Mrs. Dowson's grave in the old Easington Cemetery. One thing I remember about Mrs. Dowson was that she had an old ugly greyhound that would lie on the rug in front of the fireplace and every time you moved he would move to check you out.

Our vacation was over and we walked back down the hills that we had climbed up the week prior from the train station. The trip back to Woodbridge was just as long. You would no sooner get going and you would have to stop for another little village. Grandma had sent a care package back with us and one of the items in it was a fresh chicken that young Ralph had brought back from the farm the day before we left. One thing about Grandma was that she could really cook, but with seven boys and girls to feed, I guess she had plenty of practice.

SEVEN

During March, Dad had more authority in what he did on the base. He was given the authority to run and taxi an F84F. Dad still continued to work as assistant hanger chief. The hanger that he worked in was at the end of the base, and it was the only one that existed for the four years that we were at Woodbridge.

When you left the hanger, you could turn right and go out to the flight line. When they built the base, they separated the flight line from the hanger in case the Germans bombed it. They had built the hanger for the war so they could get a few of the planes in it along with their crews. I can remember standing by the taxi strip and Dad would taxi by sitting in the seat of a F84F. Most of the planes at Woodbridge were Korean vintage, but in 1955, the Korean conflict had only been over for two years.

The base of Woodbridge was laid out between a forest and the heather. In the heather, there were bomb craters that were left over from the Germans during World War II. The runway had the forest on one end of it. If you threw the landing bearer when you were coming in over the forest and happened to run out of runway, you would have wound up on a road that went to the base.

The flight line had a big fence around it. An AP always went around in the AP blue van. The thing that always struck me as funny was that the base chapel was right over the fence from the flight line and every time a jet started up the Chaplain office would shake. Across the road from the chapel was the base dump. One day we kids found a box of night sticks that were used by the AP. We should have kept them, but we tuned them in and all hell broke loose. I remember the leutenant sitting across the desk asking me how the hell we got them out of supply. Before I could answer, Mom was telling the leutenant that nobody swore at her son and nobody called him a liar. Well, he finally believed us after three boys were able to tell the same identical story. I bet that cocky leutenant is a fat cop in some little town by now.

The mail room was just a little building that had one door on it with some guy standing on the other side of the window making like he was God. Right next to that was base headquarters. Across the road from headquarters, was the base theater and service club. The one building that I spent a lot of time in was the service club. Some of the airmen would object to us kids being in there until they found out who our dads were.

The spring of 1956 was setting in and our Cub Scout pack had a cookout in Bentwaters. We roasted hot dogs tht were partly green when you took them out of the package from being thawed out. The marshmallows were so hard that when you put them on the stick to roast, you broke it. Like anything in the Air Force, the flight line was close enough that it drowned out anybody talking. In 1956, I met a boy that lived in Felixstowe. His dad was a sergeant at Bentwaters and he (Bob Fletcher) and I became good friends. We used to play catch and he would come out to our house and cause havoc with some of the English kids by us. We used to enjoy playing down at the local farms, especially in the haystacks with the girls. I will always remember this sixteen year old English blonde. She taught me a few things. As quiet as Bobby was, he needed two to teach him.

School got out without too many hitches. I guess the highlight of fourth grade was passing into fifth grade. The book report for the year was on <u>Treasure Island</u>.

Uncle Pete came to Bromesville in a land rover from Colchester to help me build a fort out in the heather and woods.

Special Highlights of 1955

Leaving New York for England on June 11, 1955.

Arriving in England on June 19, 1955.

Arriving at Woodbridge Air Force Base on June 21, 1955.

Meeting Uncle Paul on a hill in Edgware on Jervas Road.

Attending Charmain's Baptism.

Having Grandpa Dawson visit us at Bromesville.

Plane crash at Woodbridge when the F84 pilot was killed.

Moved to Felixstowe from Bromesville.

In the summer when our cousins, Barbara and Brian, went swimming with us in the English channel for the first time.

Spending our first Christmas in Felixstowe.

EIGHT

During the summer of 1956, I worked at the farm with Josh and played in the old fort in the harbor of Felixstowe. It was a fort built in the channel opening that ran up to Harwich Harbor.

While I would be working, Paul and Veronica would be playing in the backyard of the house. The yard had a fence around it and gooseberry bushes in the back. Paul and Veronica used to make big forts out of boxes they got from the grocery store just at the end of the street.

During that summer, we had some of our relatives visit us. We took them to the beach in Felixstowe. The beach was full of rock and not normal sand.

I used to meet Betty Sue down on the beach and we used to walk for hours. We would sit under the pier that had fishermen and a few small rides on it. We used the underside of the pier to visit real close with each other. Betty and I spent hour after hour under the pier talking about how we were going to spend the rest of our lives together. Once in awhile it would be like attending a school reunion because every other Bentwaters' department school kid would be down there watching us older kids. The British bobby would stop down and tell us kids to go on back to America and leave Felixstowe alone.

During the summer, I ran with the Jackson boys. They were brothers in a large family. Their father was a baker at Bentwaters' mess hall. He was also the baker that baked Paul's sixth birthday cake. The Jackson boys were pretty small guys, but they sure loved to fight. They were always bailing me out of some scrape. I think they just waited for me to get in a fight so they could have some fun. I remember one day Mose was getting punched, and out of nowhere, Red flew out and laid this guy out who was bigger than me.

Just about every Sunday morning, Dad and I would get up and polish our Ford. Then after our big dinner, we would go for a ride over the English countryside. My love for England's history grew more and more, ranging from the Romans to World War II. Sometimes we would have a picnic lunch on the end of an old World War II runway or maybe a Roman castle courtyard.

One particular Sunday we took a drive. We went to the base that Dad was stationed at Thurleigh near Bedford. At the time, I did not realize why we went there, but thirty years later I realized why. It was the home of the 306 BS B17 during World War II. In 1956, it was off limits but Dad found an old runway and we ate lunch there. Years later, Dad told me about taking off this runway in his B17. Now it is an experimental secret air base for the RAF (Royal Air Force). Thurleigh base bombers used to get to Germany and France and they were the first American group to bomb Germany during World War II. Dad was stationed in Thurleigh from 1942 until 1946. Looking at this base today makes your mind run wild with imagination of the sounds of an engine running and ambulances chasing after damaged aircraft and running after the wounded.

There was a sea coast beach a few miles up north from Felixstowe called Yarmouth. We used to drive up there. It was the only white sandy beach that I could remember. The ride up to Yarmouth was always more interesting then the beach. We would drive past these old fighter bases where some of the hangers and buildings were still standing. In some of these fields you could still see anti-aircraft guns and pill boxes. Usually nearby was a hole in the ground made by a bomb or plane crashing. In Suffolk there were a lot of fighter bomber bases in World War II. My biggest regret was that I did not get more pictures and record more reports. One unique thing along the English Channel was all of the radar screen directors. They were used to detect German aircraft during World War II. They now have updated the system and still use it today.

Between Lowestoft and Yarmouth there was another big shipping harbor. Many ships used to come in to load up and ship out to all parts of the world.

There were remains of an old castle just south of Lowestoft. All that was left was the outside wall and lookout towers. It was so big that farmers farmed the fields inside of the castle.

Outside the city limits of Woodbridge, there was a horse track that was used for steeple chasing. That was another place we would go to on the weekends. To this day this is the only type of horse racing I enjoy watching. The riders would sometimes fall off when jumping over a hedge and the horse would continue to run through the race. Sometimes that horse would be the first one to finish the race!

In the summer of 1956, we would go over to New Harlow to visit Uncle Paul and his family. Every time we were half an hour from Paul's house, Veronica would get sick. In fact, I can still see Dad having to stop on a curve and Veronica jumping out of the car and running to the bushes to puke. Sometimes when we would get to Paul's, we would go out to the country and have a picnic with him, June, and Charmain. When Paul moved to Harlow, there was a creek behind their house that had a little wooden bridge over it. One day, I got into a fight with a kid that years later ended up playing with the music group called the Rolling Stones. He lived next to Paul (his mother still lives there). We used to play cricket and soccer behind Paul's house, but now there are garages and a field full of gypsies. In those days there weren't any McDonald's, so Dad and Paul would walk up to the top of the small shopping center, have a beer, and bring back some fish and chips for us to eat. Dad's favorite pub was *The Hair*. Paul and Dad would walk up to the top of the hill to go to the Pub for a pint of beer then go across the street to the best fish and chips shop in the world. (In 1985, our son Jim sat and drank beer with us in a salute to Mom and Dad. The doors were very short and Jim was 6'6" and had to duck about a foot to get in the building. Even our twelve year old son Jon had to duck to enter with us).

Harlow is a very old town. It's history goes back to the Roman times. There are not many remains left, but when they start to build new houses they have to check with the local historical society to see if they would be digging up any ruins. In 1956, Harlow was just beginning to grow with industries and special businesses coming in from London. Many have doubled in size now.

Back in Felixstowe we would spend a lot of time in old World War II camps. I guess our favorite thing to do back then was to see who could spot a Navy ship coming up the Harwich Harbor Canal.

I'll never forget the day we were playing by the old fort and all of the sudden a ship went up the river with a Japanese emblem on it. It was being chased by a British Navy destroyer. We watched a small ship come up behind both of them. There was a lot of smoke coming from the guns but we could not see any shells landing. By this time we were all getting scared. One English boy started crying and ran home. We started to head up the dirt road and a bunch of Jeeps and Army trucks went by us. Suddenly, a jeep pulled up by us and a guy in civilian clothes jumped out screaming at us in English, "You are interfering with my movie!" As it turned out, a movie company had rented out the farmland, canal and harbor to make a movie. The supervisor of the movie then came up in a truck loaded with cameras and talked to us a little nicer. He told us that we could watch, but only from the fields on the eastside of the road. The following day the road was closed to the public. I can still see me and three of my English friends crawling along the hedges through fence lines as if we were going to attack these 'Japs'. We spent the whole day watching these guys dressed like English and Japanese soldiers shooting at each other.

We stayed there until dark and watched the lights set up and campfires started in the Japanese camps. In England it does not get dark very early. Our game for that night was to get up the road without getting caught by the movie company. That day we didn't get into trouble with the movie group, but I sure got hell from Mom for not coming home for lunch or supper.

After the movie company left, old Josh sat in his living room after tea and told us kids what it was really like to be in the war. He said the Germans in World War I were worse than the Japs. One thing Josh told us about that movie was that the 'Japs' wouldn't have camped so close to the English without shooting or attacking them. Also, he said that the Japanese had different Jeeps than us. While shooting the movie, they were using borrowed World War II American Jeeps.

NINE

Somehow we managed to make it through the summer. Some things that were done that summer are not printable so that I may protect my family and friends. Besides, if my Mom had known half of the things that I had done, I probably would have had more than just bad feet.

The first day of school that year started real great. I got on the bus and found some guy sitting next to Betty Sue. He was smaller than me and I thought he was younger than me so I told him to move because he was sitting next to my girl. He told me to "buzz off" so I went and sat down behind him and Betty and annoyed him all the way to Bentwaters. When we got to school the AP that was assigned to the bus grabbed me and told me that I was going to the principal's office. I walked in with him, and not knowing the new guy, I had to tell him my name. He looked at his list, smiled and said, "Oh yes, Mike Byrd. I know all about you! You were a problem last year, but you will not be this year." I told him about the kid who was sitting in the seat that was assigned to me last year. He then told me that was last year and if I was going to be a problem that I would have to sit in the front of the bus. I pleaded with the principal and he and the AP finally agreed to allow me to have the seat I had last year.

After I left the principal's office, I set out to find this new kid that was moving in on my territory. I managed to find Mose and Red Jackson. After telling them what had happened they said, "Let's get him, Byrd"! We found the red-headed kid and took him to an old bomb shelter where we spent a lot of time that was still on the playground. While we were proceeding to persuade him to leave my girl alone, up stepped a short, pudgy red haired teacher who then proceeded to take us to the principal's office. The principal said, "Byrd, twice in less than thirty minutes? I can see this is going to be a long year." We all got our asses chewed out and assigned to the office during recess for the first week of school. Then to make things worse, I went to class and who was sitting in the teacher's desk but the short, pudgy teacher with red hair. Mose looked back at me and his eyes were the size of baseballs. He said, "Byrd, this ain't going to be a good year." I remember adding that it was not going to be easy. Just before we got the empty desks that were in the back of the room, the little red head teacher (Mr. Ryan) said, "Well, if it isn't the boxing team! You two are in the front of the room so I can keep you guys clean."

That had to be the hardest day of my thirteen years in school with two trips to the principal's office in one day and no recess. On the bus on the way home, Mose and I passed a note back and forth making a plan to get back at this kid for making our day so rotten (I still can't remember his name). We decided to invite him to the beach on Saturday morning for a game of football. I remember Betty telling me that we were going to make things worse. I accused her of liking the twerp and she told me that she didn't but she just didn't want me to get hurt.

We got the football game organized on the beach next to the Felixstowe pier. It was Saturday morning at 10:00 a.m. The Jackson boys and I showed up along with the little troublemaker and four other kids we allowed him to bring. The one thing that was nice was that the beach was all rocks and pebbles with little or no sand. We played pretty good for a few plays, then we got the ball. The play was designed so that I would carry the ball and Red would block for me. When Red got down in front of me, he picked up a rock and when he went to block the kid in front of him, we were going to split the kid's forehead open. The fight began. I wound up on top of this kid's head kicking him in the back. A couple of fishermen had to come and break up the fight. Red, Mose, and I said that the other kids started it. The English guy said that we shouldn't have fought and then told us that we should take the lad home and get him some aid. We started to take the kid home. We got around the first bend and then told the kid to get lost and we took off toward the roller coaster rides.

Monday came around and I got on the bus. There was a new AP on the bus and since we were the last ones to get on I hurried to get the seat next to Betty so that the kid would get stuck sitting next to the AP. I sat down next to Betty Sue and Veronica said, "Remember Mike, Mom said that you better behave or you will get a spanking and sent to bed without any supper." Everybody on the bus looked at me and started laughing. Veronica had a way of making me look like shit.

Mr. Ryan was a very strict teacher. During the year he had to take some time off because we were too hard on him. Some people said it was a vacation but I said it was a nervous breakdown.

During the fall, I worked hard on my cub scouting and by March 1957 I had received my 'arrow of light'. I remember working on a silly electrical project for a display. It ran at home, but when I set it up at the pack meeting it wouldn't even buzz.

Our junior high football team did a pretty good job winning games. Most of the games were played at the other bases. Sometimes the games were cancelled because the buses couldn't move and the bases were on alert due to thick fog. I tried to go to as many games as possible because I figured by my seventh grade year, I would be the star end. As it turned out, I was the star of the end of the bench.

As the year went by there was talk of my dad getting a house on the base. The orders finally came through and we were going to live on the base at 1010B in January.

In the fall, the English celebrate "Guy Fox" Day. They build bonfires and light firecrackers off. Our family was out driving that night and somebody threw a firecracker at our car. One of my friends was standing on the corner when it happened and ran over and started to fight with the kid who threw the firecracker. The next thing we knew, half the block was fighting. Dad drove away undamaged.

Christmas of 1956 was another big shipment from Sears. I remember Dad bringing home all the presents from the base post office. I think that Mom ordered them back in August. My big present that year was my first stamp collection book. It was a green book that my folks had bought in downtown Felixstowe. It still has a turkey stamp in it that I glued back in 1956. Mom knitted each of us a pair of gloves except Paul because he was so little he needed mittens. I still remember that they were grey.

It was cold that year in December and we wondered if it was going to snow for Christmas, but it didn't. I walked to the butcher's shop on Christmas Eve to pick up our turkey. It was freshly killed and plucked. I had to carry that big bird home and Mom made me put it in a brown shopping bag just in case I dropped it. I thought that bird weighed a ton!

Christmas dinner consisted of Mom's specially baked turkey, potatoes, Brussels sprouts, and Yorkshire pudding. We all had bonbons which were popped and then we wore the hats. I can still see the smiles on Mom's and Dad's faces. Christmas in England was always very happy. Paul always came up with something funny even if it was just the way he wore his clothes. Usually his house coat was only half buttoned.

Today, people shop with credit cards but to this day I still can't figure out how our parents had the money to pay for everything we had.

The day after Christmas we packed things up for our move to the base in Woodbridge. Mom kept saying that she wanted everything ready for the movers. They weren't coming until the twentieth of January!

We spent time playing on the farm. Old Josh had retired and the rotten red-headed Irishman had taken over. I also have memories of our last time playing at the fort at the harbor. There were two other boys that I had met at the bike races that summer. We had just gotten off our bikes, and all of the sudden we were jumped by six other guys. They chased us all the way up the hill to the old army base where they were greeted by some of our other friends. All hell broke loose! It was a great fight! I remember seeing a kid get hit on the head with a stick and when he hit the ground he didn't move. The next thing we knew, there was an old farmer swearing at us and telling us to quit killing each other. We took off toward our bikes and just as I went to jump on mine the copper grabbed me and said, "O.K., yank, where do you think you're going?" He questioned us for about thirty minutes and found that we hadn't started the fight, but we managed to finish it. The kid that was hurt had to be taken home by the copper so his parents could get him medical care. I never did see any of these kids again. We moved to the base and I never got back to Felixstowe to see my buddies again.

Just before we moved, some CO decided to have an alert, so Dad had to rush off for the base. The day was a typical foggy day and the roads were icy. Dad told us when he went up a big hill that we called snake hill, the car started to slide. By the time he arrived at the base, the alert had been cancelled because the planes weren't able to get off of the ground due to the fog.

TEN

The big day finally came—moving day. A big truck came to our house in Felixstowe and began to load our furniture. All of our friends came to see us off. Even some of the guys that did not like me stopped by to say "bye, yank." Looking back now, I think they wanted to make sure that we were leaving.

On the afternoon of January 21, 1957, we turned up the road to our new house on the base in Woodbridge. Our house number was 1010B until we came back to the States in 1959. The first thing I remember about that house was that instead of a fireplace, we had a furnace. All of the furniture in the house was new. Paul and I had a room in the front part of the house and Veronica's room was in the back. Our kitchen had a washer and dryer as well as all of the other conveniences. The house had a nice big living room and dining room. It was built up on a sandy hill so there wasn't any grass. Mom even hired a guy to plant grass, but it never came up. Our house was at the end of the street. The CO decided which of the most important airmen would get the first available house, and Dad got one. The first row of houses had everyone from the AP sergeant to the fire sergeant. The houses were built like duplexes. Msgt. McQuerries lived in 1010A and at night Paul and I would bang on the wall and Steve and Terry would bang back at us.

On the first day of school we all walked down to the bus stop that was in the big parking lot behind Sergeant Hyden's house. We thought that we would get new buses, but as things go, we wound up with the same buses and a tougher AP. Bentwaters' AP force was small but a close group. When I stepped on to the bus, the AP said "good morning" so I thought he was a nice guy. My opinion quickly changed. When we all were loaded on the bus, the AP stepped on, adjusted his white hat, stood at attention, and proceeded to introduce himself. Some kid laughed in the middle of the bus and the big AP walked up to him and asked him what was so funny and then moved him to the front of the bus.

Once we were settled in, I had the nightly duty of walking our dog, Bella. One night we were walking on what I thought was a road, but suddenly we fell three feet into a trench almost choking poor Bella.

After advancing from Cub Scouts to Boy Scouts, I remember the big arrow of light ceremony. I couldn't figure out what the guys dressed up like Indians were doing there. Now, after thirty years, I know. Our Boy Scout troop had their own building and base even gave a special part of the woods to the Boy Scouts. It was off limits to anyone else except the Boy Scouts.

Mr. Ryan turned out to be a pretty good teacher. He worked with me quite a bit since I was having trouble in school. When spring came around, he rotated back to the States and passed me on to the sixth grade. Before school let out, the base had Little League tryouts. I had never played baseball before, so I learned how to outfield and Mr. Ryan taught me how to throw the ball. One day, he was working with me and when we got done, he autographed the baseball that we were using. To this day, I still have that ball with his name on it. The ball is with the trophy that I later won with the Tigers' Little League team for becoming Bentwaters' Little League champs. Mr. Ryan was a good disciplinarian, but he was always willing to help us guys that were looking for trouble.

Before school got out in the spring, I would go down to Mr. Cooper's store before getting on the bus in the morning and I would charge ice cream sandwiches. It worked great until Mike, the guy who worked for Mr. Cooper's store, came around with the monthly milk bill. Mom asked what the sandwiches were for and Mike told her I was charging them. Bang! Mom back-handed me across the side of my face and knocked me at least three feet. She was small but she carried the strength of the Guns of Naveron. Mom got the mess straightened out, but it left my parents short for the month. Before I knew it, I was working for Mr. Cooper's store delivering milk, eggs and bread with Mike. I would start work at about 6:00 a.m. delivering milk to the NCO and officers' quarters on Woodbridge. Then at about noon we would go over to Bentwaters to deliver milk and bread to the officers' quarters. Sometimes we would have a cheeseburger and fries from the officers' club. Mike had a buddy that worked at the club who would sneak them out the back door. I don't remember what Mike would give him, but once in awhile I would get a pack of cigarettes for him. To this day, those were the best cheeseburgers and fries I've ever had.

During June, our troop went to Camp Mohawk to go camping for a week. Our tents that we used were two man walls with wooden floors in them. Also, our cooking was only done when we went camping away from camp for a night. Otherwise we marched to the mess hall singing our troop song (which was something like "hold your head high 277 is passing by"). When we went out for our night camping outing, I had diarrhea and shit my pants. I remember throwing them into the woods. All of us new Scouts were initiated into the troops. We were stripped and taken into the woods and then black-balled. I remember telling my mom about this when we got back home and was she ever pissed! She even raised hell with the Scout Master. We didn't see anything wrong with it. Anyway, I bought a t-shirt with a Camp Mohawk Indian on it, made some beads, got homesick, cried in my sleep, fell in the shower trying to wash the charcoal off my balls, managed to have some fun, and I still didn't learn how to swim.

There was a camp counselor, although I don't recall his name, but his younger brother was in our troop camping with us at Mohawk for the very first time. This counselor went crazy one night. The staff chased him all over camp trying to catch him. They told us Scouts to stay in our campsites and not leave. After awhile, an air force ambulance arrived from one of the nearby bases. They tied him up in a straight jacket, and left their lights and siren on their way to Wimpole Park which was about 2.5 hours away.

When we left Camp Mohawk to return to Woodbridge, we went past Stonehenge. I thought "what a strange piece of stone work." Later in school I read what it was. Once back to Woodbridge, I resumed the summer activities of working for Mr. Cooper, doing things with the Scouts, and raising a little hell with the APs.

As the baseball season came to an end, our team, the Tigers, won the championship at Woodbridge and Bentwaters. When it was the playoff game, I came down with the mumps and had some complications with them. I got hives and my eyes swelled shut. The base doctor restricted me to my bed at home. Everyday he would come to our house and give me a shot. To this day, I don't know what the shot was for.

During this time, the 79th was TDY in Africa getting our new planes. They were F100 super-sabers. With me being sick, the base doctor called the CO in Africa and had Dad come home early. The story goes, the night before Dad was due to come home, he was in the shower and there were two other guys in there. A pilot said that he had to fly this sergeant back to Woodbridge because he had a sick kid. He said, "Man, am I ever going to give that sergeant the ride of his life!" The other guy that was in the shower said, "Look, lieutenant, you might be able to get the sergeant and plane up in the air, but keep your plane up there and get it back safe on the ground!" As Dad walked out, he told the pilot to have a safe trip. The next morning, Dad was out at the plane waiting for the pilot. When the pilot showed up, Dad saluted him and said, "Sergeant Byrd reporting for flight to Woodbridge." I guess the look on the pilot's face was something to behold. The pilot and Dad walked around the plane inspecting it. As they walked, the pilot said "well, it is the pilot's job to fly us safe and I know you have this plane in top shape so I won't give you the ride of your life as I said last night."

Back at Woodbridge, I was in bed when the phone rang. Mom came in my bedroom and said that my father would be landing in fifteen minutes. The next thing I knew, there was a roar of a jet passing over the base which rattled all of the windows. Mom then said that Dad was coming home in a new jet with some hot dog rookie pilot.

When Dad arrived home, a CO had a staff car to bring him to our house. When Dad got unpacked he put an African hat on my head. I could not see it until my eyes opened up a few days later. During my illness, my Little League team had beat my best friends' team in the Little League Championship at Bentwaters. We had an award ceremony at the officer club at Bentwaters. I remember our coach when he called everyone up for our trophies. When it came to my turn, he just said, "Byrd you have one. Aren't you going to come get it?" This was for me (the guy who had never got a hit all year, but made some outstanding catches in right field!) I remember that after our first game win, our coach bought us hamburgers and Cokes at the service club. He said every game we won he would buy us burgers and Cokes. After the first month we had a coaching change. I don't know why he quit but the base CO covered the tab for the rest of the year at the service club for our team.

During the season we went to Lakenheath and played one of their teams. Their pitcher was John Livingston (later that year, John's dad was stationed at Bentwaters and we became good friends). We beat Lakenheath and when we were leaving the base somebody chased us down because they found a glove and thought that it might be one of our players. When we got back to Woodbridge, the CO took us down to the service club to feed us. One thing about the Air force in the 50's is that they sure treated their dependent's ball teams great!

The Tigers were made up of a bunch of guys that came together with a lot of hard luck. They were a great squadron to represent and win the championship. I can still see the parade they gave us when we started the season. It covered the whole base and even some movie stars came to the opening. I remember they called my name and I walked out between first and home for the introduction of our team. We beat the Yankees that day.

The summer came to an end and we all went back to school. Mr. Coon was my new teacher during September. I met an airman that was in charge of the recreation hall. He printed the base paper and I delivered it.

Our Base Entrance Sign 79th

Champs, 1957, Tigers Little League, Bentwater and Woodbridge

Bentwaters 1958 Thunderbird Armed Forces Day

Grandma Dawson. My Grandmother in Loftus backyard, 1955

This is the kid that was sitting next to Betty Sue on the school bus. He is the kid that the Jackson boys and I had a fight with at school.

Jr. High football at Bentwaters, 1958. Base motor pool in background. Me last on the left.

Me going camping. My cookgear and canteen, extra food in bag.
My bike in front of our house 1010B, 1958

Mom in background, our Great Aunt Lou in front, 1956, at Aunt
Lou's house.

Felixstowe Beach, note the rocky beach. Front row, left to right: Paul, a cousin, Veronica, Me   Back row: Mom and cousins.

Christmas at Woodbridge 1958

Thunderbirds 1958 Bentwaters. They are F-100s

Re-fueler and 3 F-100s at Bentwater Armed Forces Day 1958

Woodbridge, 1958 on a Sunday. Left to right: Alan Shaffer, Keith Shaffer, Me, Veronica

Thunderbirds 1958 Bentwaters. They are F-100s

Re-fueler and 3 F-100s at Bentwater Armed Forces Day 1958

9 F-100s, Bentwater Armed Forces Day 1958. The Thunderbirds.

Missing Planes in Formation # 22

My report card 7th grade

PARENT - TEACHER CONFERENCE

Name .. *Mike Byrd* ....

School .. *Bentwaters* .... Grade .. *7b* ....

Teacher .. *Burnette* .... Date *7 March 1959*

AREAS OF STRENGTH:

Math   *Cooperative*
Well behaved   *Pleasant disposition*
Language

AREAS OF WEAKNESSES:

Science
Social Studies

Teacher's Plans for Child	Parent's Plans for Child
Mike is the type student that must work hard to get a passing mark. He is a well behaved student but behind in fundamentals. Burnette *55 More effort is needed — test scores remain low* *math. Mike does fair Barley work. M 9*	*J Byrd* Parent's Signature

53

My dad English driver license

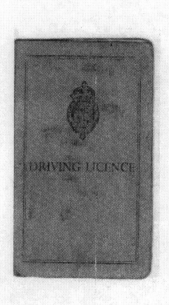

5¢ & 10¢ Scrap	Ist		1955 issue
	2nd	5¢	1955 issue
	3rd	10¢	1957 issue

79th Sqt Orders
Dad was on it

79TH TACTICAL FIGHTER SQUADRON (USAFE)
United States Air Force
APO 755, New York, New York

SPECIAL ORDERS)
NUMBER   A-46)

12 March 1959

1. MSGT BENJAMIN P CAREY, AF6900854, this organization, this station is awarded the Good Conduct Medal (Bronze with 4 loops), for his demonstration of exemplary behavior, efficiency, and fidelity during the period 9 Aug 52 to 8 Aug 55.

2. The following named airmen, this organization, this station are authorized to Run-Up and Taxi F-100 type aircraft. All PERAMS and Special Orders in conflict to this order are hereby rescinded. Authority: AFR 66-10.

GRADE, NAME, AFSN	GRADE, NAME, AFSN
MSGT EDWARD G KISSEL, AF18046323	MSGT VICTOR H SMITH, AF20428183
MSGT ZANE R HARTMAN, AF18136635	TSGT JAMES R BYRD, AF16046545
TSGT RAYMOND J DEFRESE, AF18326364	TSGT HARRY E HENRY, AF19363910
TSGT CHARLES J KELLY, AF20310093	TSGT DONALD R SNYDER, AF12244119
TSGT CARLOS STAITENBECK, AF18282320	TSGT JAMES C TENPENNY, AF7008408
TSGT JOHN P WASHLESKI, AF33188121	TSGT JACK F WILLIAMS, AF35602350
TSGT RALPH H WOLTERING, AF16239538	SSGT LEON WILLIAMS, AF13561522
SSGT JAMES E WARE, AF13476615	SSGT BILLY J LEA, AF18399525

3. The following named airmen, this organization, this station are authorized to Run-Up F-100 type aircraft. All PERAMS, and Special Orders in conflict to this order are hereby rescinded. Authority: AFR 66-10.

GRADE, NAME, AFSN	GRADE, NAME, AFSN
SSGT REGINALD W GALLASHAW, AF13345793	A/1C WILLIAM R CASE, AF19485635
A/2C CARL R ANDERSON, AF19593417	A/2C BRUCE A CRAGER, AF16539678
A/2C GARY W JOHNSTON, AF12487562	A/2C LARRY L MORRIS, AF27721023
A/2C SHELDON L NICKEL, AF13535439	A/2C RAYMOND R TEWALT, AF15557486
A/2C RAYMOND C WHITWORTH, AF14015265	A/2C TODD HILL, AF17478163
A/2C FREDERICK J MANNING, AF16508227	A/2C DONALD E MUNSON, AF16474880
A/2C JOHN C CURRY, AF16522276	A/2C ANTHONY W VITOLO, AF15552073
A/2C WAYNE CALHOUN, AF17463247	

4. The following named Airmen, this organization, this station are authorized to Trim on F-100 type aircraft. All PERAMS and orders in conflict to this Special Order are hereby rescinded. Authority: AFR 66-10.

GRADE, NAME, AFSN	GRADE, NAME, AFSN
TSGT RALPH H WOLTERING, AF16239538	TSGT DONALD R SNYDER, AF12244119
A/2C JIMMIE J THITTS, AF15589839	

5. A/3C PAUL P CAHILL, AF11336601, this organization, this station is authorized to Run-Up L-20A type aircraft. All PERAMS and Special Orders in conflict to this Special Order are hereby rescinded. Authority: AFR 66-10.

Our Housing Orders
Telling us what house and date our move

7546TH SUPPORT SQUADRON (USAFE)
United States Air Force
APO 755, USAF

LETTER ORDERS)
NUMBER   29   21 January 1957

SUBJECT: Assignment of Quarters

THRU: Commander
          79th Fighter Bomber Squadron
          APO 755, US Air Force

TO: TSGT BYRD, JAMES R, AF16046545
          79th Fighter Bomber Squadron
          APO 755, US Air Force

          Pursuant to authority contained in paragraph 4, Air Force Regulation 35-6, 10 August
1951, you are assigned government quarters, Number_____1018_____, RAF Station
Woodbridge, effective 21 January 1957

          BY ORDER OF THE COMMANDER:

                                              THEODORE G DRISCOLL, Jr
                                              1st Lt, USAF
                                              Asst Adjutant

DISTRIBUTION:
    1-Indiv concerned
    2-Indiv's Pers Off
    1-S Comm Off
    1-Fin Off
    1-AIO
    1-Housing Off, Woodbridge
    1-Housing Off, Bentwaters
    XXXXXXXXXXXXXXXXXXXXXXXXX

An art and craft show
that I was in the 3rd AF

Arts and Crafts Winners Named

Winners of the Bentwaters Arts and Crafts Contest conducted by the Base Library during February were announced this week. All entries, which have been on display for the past week in the new Base Library on Ring Road, have now been forwarded for participation in the Third Air Force 1958 Arts and Crafts Contest.

First prizes of $5.00 each were won by James G. Byrd, dependent son of T/Sgt. and Mrs. James R. Byrd, 79th Fighter Bomber Squadron, for his light oak footstool in Woodworking (Junior Youth); Mrs. Beverly A. Engelhardt, dependent wife of Capt F. A. Engelhardt, 81st Field Maintenance Sqn for her knitted child's sweater in Needlework (Adult); Lynn Kendrick, dependent daughter of M/Sgt. and Mrs. Arlyn Kendrick, 81st Field Maintenance Squadron, for her clothespin bag in Needlework (Junior Youth); Mrs. E. Holland, UK civilian of the RAF Liaison Office, for her woollen toy dog in Miscellaneous Crafts (Adult); Mr. John F. Hunter, DAF civilian in Budget and Accounting, for his oil painting "Theatre" in Art (Adult) and Roy D. Ola, dependent son of Col. and Mrs. George J. Ola, 81st Field Maintenance Sqn, for Fighter Bomber Wing, for his drawing "Oak Tree" in Art (Junior Youth). A second prize of $3.00 was also awarded Mrs. Engelhardt for her crocheted baby blanket in Needlework (Adult).

ELEVEN

Wimpole Park was an estate owned by an English family with the land temporarily assigned to the third air force hospital group. It consisted of everything pertaining to medical help. You could have a baby there right up to getting a new valve put in your heart. Along with the medical help, they had cooks, APs, and a general operation crew which kept everything else that an air force squadron would need to run.

The buildings were Quonset huts lined up in rows with halls running between the buildings which were all enclosed. You could go into the admissions office and not walk outside until you were on the other side of the hospital.

I remember the entrance gate. It had an AP standing in his sharp blue uniform, white gloves and those white leggings (which they had to bleach every time they took them off). The entrance had two stone posts on both sides of the road. When they closed down the base and tore down the building, these posts were all that was left of the base. I have been back to England three times and have never been able to find them.

The base had a baseball team. I never saw them play, but in 1992 in Nashville, Tennessee, we attended a reunion for the Wimpole Park Hospital group and met some of the players.

When I was admitted into the hospital, I was assigned to ward three. It was the orthopedic ward. When I walked in the ward, they put me in a private room. They said I was too young to be on the ward with airmen (even though I had spent 85% of my time with them). They would play cards--they even tried to teach me. I think some of the games were Hearts and Pee-knuckle. There was one game that they played with a board with holes in it which had all kinds of little pegs. It wasn't until years later that I found out it was called Cribbage.

On a Saturday afternoon while I was in my room, I heard a loud noise. It was coming from a man in a bed who was screaming in pain. He had his leg up in the air on top of a splint hanging in his bed. They had him hooked up to an IV and pint of plasma. I went down the hall to watch and all of the sudden there was a voice behind me saying, "Jimmy! Get back in your room!" I turned around and there was my "Mom." "Mom" wasn't my real mother but rather the little captain nurse that everyone on the ward called "Mom."

The day I had my surgery, "Mom" stayed with me. My real mom and dad had made the decision not to be there because they were told that I would be sleeping from the either. Instead, it made me sick. I can still see that yellow-green shit coming from my mouth while "Mom" held the puke pan. To this day, I am not sure of this sweet nurse's name. (Gladys sticks in my mind, but I'm not sure).

Well, we lived through the first day after surgery. They had my whole left leg in a cast that was bent at the knee. "Mom" had given her duties to a tall, good-looking nurse who was to stay with me. On the second day, Mom and Dad came to see me. They brought me a gift. It was some apples and oranges. I still didn't want anything to eat. My gut hurt more than my leg. Dad was sitting at the end of my bed when somebody knocked on my room door, walked in, and asked my dad if he was Sergeant Byrd. When he found out that he indeed was who he thought, the man introduced himself (whose name I have forgotten) and explained he was a fireman from Woodbridge and was one of the fellows who had played on our baseball team for the 79th. He had asked my dad that, if on his next visit, he would bring some gear for him from his barracks (this man was in for a shoulder injury from playing baseball).

As for my leg, I began to get accustomed to the heavy cast. My first week after surgery was spent in bed. Back in those days it was customary--you stayed in bed. I look at medical care now and the rush to get you up and going amazes me. After the first week, the first thing I did was to find a toilet and sit on it for a half an hour (bedpans are not the most pleasant with a twenty pound cast). I can still hear that orderly knocking on my door asking if I was O.K. or if I had fallen in.

During my recuperation, I made several trips to the hobby shop. I would ask Mom if I could go and I would always have to wait until someone would go with me because I was in a wheelchair. Once in awhile, I would go to the base theater with some of the other airmen. I remember we would go down dark halls waiting for someone to open a door and hit us. The guys would always put me in front because if a door did open, it would catch the big wooden wheel on my chair. They always would have some joke, especially if it would be a young nurse coming out to go to her barracks.

I remember that there was an old sergeant who was confined to his bed. One day a lady came to see him. I heard noises and investigated and found that it was not his wife. A few days later when his wife came to visit him, (although I don't remember what I said) my mouth must have been faster than my brain because I got the sergeant in trouble with his wife. I remember that before it was all over, I was back in my room and he and his wife were in a private room trying to make up. After the fireworks had cooled down, I told the sergeant I was sorry and didn't think I was going to get him in trouble. His only response was, "Someday kid, it will happen to you." Ten years later, I had to agree with him. It did happen to me.

A second lieutenant was admitted one day. I don't remember his problem, but he was having issues with going to the bathroom. He was complaining about it and not cooperating with the nurses. The nurses finally had it with him and gave him the old catheter trick. On another day, the word got out that we were going to have a GI party. I thought it would be cake and pop--wrong! It was a scrub brush and a pail. The patients were required to clean up our ward. I remember lying over my bed and dusting the mop board. When the inspector came through the next morning, he never came into my room. Typical air force "clean it up and I won't look."

When it came time for me to get my stitches out, I wouldn't let the medic take them out. I thought Dr. Fetgerld put my stitches in and he was going to be the one to take them out. So one Saturday, instead of going to town, Dr. Fetgerld came in and took them out. I watched him as he turned on this saw that I thought was going to cut my leg off. It vibrated so much that I thought I was going to bounce off the bed. I was hanging on the side of the bed waiting for the pain to begin when all of the sudden the doctor was over at the sink mixing up plaster to patch up where he had cut my cast. I thought that it was going to hurt but I never felt a thing. Dr. Fetgerld was an orthopedic surgeon. He was a captain and I never really got to know him, but he did ride with us in the same plane in 1959 back to the United States. I think he was from Chicago. I have never been able to find him, but maybe one day our paths will cross and he will show up at one of the reunions.

The most exciting thing that happened was on a weekend. There was a guy who was in our ward that was always giving some airmen shit. I saw two airmen standing on one side of the ward, and the second lieutenant was sitting in his wheelchair out in front of the door that went outside. At this particular time, the door was open. The two airmen walked up and pushed the southern accented mouthy lieutenant off the platform and down the two cement steps. There were words exchanged as I sat there laughing. Then an orderly showed up yelling at us. I was still laughing when "Mom" came running in and was screaming at us. She knew it wasn't me that had done this to the Lieutenant, but none the less, no one was owning up to who did it, so everyone was restricted to bed. I was sent to my room. The next thing I knew, there were a couple of AP's walking down the hall with another guy. I don't think that lieutenant ever found out who pushed him, because everyone that was questioned said they never saw a thing. To this day, I am not sure who really did it.

In the meantime, it was getting close to Thanksgiving and our ward received some pictures colored by some department school students. I got to looking at them and some of the names looked familiar, when I came across one that had my sister Veronica's name on it. I asked the airman who had it if he would swap. He said it didn't make any difference to him so I took Veronica's picture and gave him the one I had.

I knew I was getting out pretty soon. They had taught me how to walk on crutches so I knew the hospital was getting ready to discharge me. After six weeks of me, they had enough. When my parents came to pick me up, they had a present for "Mom" since she had helped me so much. It was a clock. My parents had used some money that I had earned from delivering the base newspaper to pay for it. When I gave "Mom" the clock, I can remember her saying that she would always keep it to remind her of me. Discharge time was upon us and we went down to admissions, but before they would let me go, they wanted some money for all the trips to the hobby shop. Then they said the food I had eaten had to be paid for. Thank goodness that was all they had to pay because the air force had paid for all the medical expenses. I remember my mom getting mad when I said that I didn't eat all the food because I had been sick for a few days. Goodbyes were said to everyone. I did not get to see any more of the people when I went back for a check-up. I guess they were all off duty. We did pass "Mom" going out the main gate.

It wasn't until 1992 in Nashville, Tennessee that I got to see some of the people that worked on me and had done some of my paperwork. It was my chance to tell them thank you for what they had done for me.

TWELVE

My first day back at school was a treat in itself. I asked Mr. Coon what kind of back homework I had. He said I just had to pass a test and behave in class. Well, I passed some, but I did behave in class.

Our family got ready for Christmas. My grandmother and uncles, Graham and Adrain, came and spent some time with us. The big thing about Christmas was trying to open my presents with a big cast on my leg. I also remember that every time I went walking down the road, I would slip on the ice with my crutches.

The year 1957 ended and I had accomplished three major things:
Joined Boy Scouts.
Played Little League.
Had my fourth foot operation.

Major Events from 1957:
Move to Woodbridge 1010B.
Got in trouble for charging ice cream sandwiches at Mr. Coopers.
Started to work for Mr. Cooper helping haul milk.
Started to play Little League in May.

Joined troop 277 in April.

Went to Camp Mohawk in July.

79th went to Tripple.

79th got F-100.

October through November had foot operation.

F86 crashed at the end of the runway at Bentwaters and the pilot was killed.

Sold candy bars at Woodbridge gym for Troop 277.

Went to visit Uncle Paul quite a bit.

Went to Grandma's house in Yorkshire.

Spent Sunday nights at church watching films and eating the best sweet rolls that I can remember.

Playing in the old dump.

Always trying to get stamps from the postman at the base post office.

The base commander kept pulling alerts.

Fog caused the Stars and Stripes not to be delivered to the base.

Got Bella in Yorkshire.

THIRTEEN

1958

During the winter of 1958, I kept the medic busy at the base hospital repairing my cast that I kept breaking. I remember one day Whitney, the medic, said, "It ain't going to be long Byrd, and you won't be able to lift your leg." Bobby Fletcher must have put ten pounds of muscle on his body by carrying my books back and forth from my house to the bus. Don't get me wrong, but I did average one book a week that I would take home.

During the winter, I kept my arms in shape by walking on my crutches and squeezing my rubber golf ball. I wanted to get my arm back in shape to pitch Little League in May.

Easter came and Dad had another fifteen day leave. We were going to go to Grandma's house but the doctor did not remove my cast so we couldn't travel. My Uncle Graham came to visit us instead. During his visit, we spent a lot of time doing things on the base. I used to go to Bentwaters on Saturday mornings to watch my friends bowl at the ally and the Woodbridge base basketball team at the gym. I kept very busy on my crafts and Boy Scouts. I did not really work hard at anything.

Our Scout troop sold Hershey candy bars at the basketball games. All I did was sit by the full boxes and pass them out to the Scouts that were selling in the stands. Our troop really did not have to sell to raise money because the Air Force provided us with everything we needed, but we did anyway.

Woodbridge's basketball team did not do very well in 1958. Their biggest rivals were Bentwater and Weathersfield.

Spring rolled around and my folks took me to Wimpole Park on a Monday for a check-up which held the possibility of getting my cast removed. Dr. Fetgerld decided to cut my cast off, x-ray my foot, and gave me a shot in the back of my foot. He then told me to go home and start walking with the crutches for a week and then throw them away. I then said goodbye to the personnel at Wimpole Park and left for spring training at Woodbridge Little League baseball field. It was on a Saturday, just twelve days after my cast was removed, that I was playing in my first game of baseball in the year 1958.

I was put on the Braves team, which made my dad pretty happy since the Milwaukee Braves had won the World Series in 1957. Mr. Brown was our coach and also our school principal. We started out really well, losing our first two games. After every game, Mr. Brown would post our batting average on the post that was in the hallway of the school. I held the bottom place for batting with only one hit. During practice they tried to teach me how to catch. I thought it was bad enough to pitch, but not catch. I played left field and caught a few balls. I remember running into the fence to catch one and heaving myself over it.

Also during this summer I lost my love for baseball and concentrated on earning money for Mr. Cooper.

Armed Forces Day came in May and our Scout troop marched with all the big guys from the end of the flight line halfway up the runway at Bentwaters. After we were done, we got to watch the rest of the parade. Man, was the third Air Force band sharp. They then cleaned up the runway and the fly boys took over. The KC133 flew over with two F-100 and two F-101 planes from the 79th and 81st. After the jets cleared the air there was a little applause. All of the sudden, we heard a different sound. Looking up into the sun we could see that there was a little propeller plane coming at us. Bob Fletcher was standing next to me and he said it was a P51 and I said that I thought it was an English plane, the Spitfire. Ironically, it was the last Spitfire flying for the RAF. It landed and taxied up to the FLT line where it was on display for the rest of the show. I forgot what rank the pilot was, but he sure had ribbons hanging on his chest. I remember he told us that he had flown this same plane and had shot down twelve German planes during the Battle of Britain. When we looked at the Spitfire closer, we noticed that there were a lot of patches in the fuselage.

There was suddenly a lot of clapping and yelling so we looked up to see what was going on. It was the Thunderbirds. There were eight F100s. It was my first time ever seeing the Thunderbirds. They were the Air Force's best, but being a kid of twelve years, I thought the 79th F100 were the best. Besides our yellow tigers looked better than those birds they had painted on their tails.

Back then it was O.K. to break the sound barrier. One of the Thunderbirds did a low level high speed pass and rocked the ground. People today would have been calling the FAA with a complaint. The neatest thing was when two Thunderbirds flew at each other one was upside down and the other was right side up. Then they tried it again. The plane that was supposed to fly upside down started to roll over on his back. One wing hit the ground and caused the plane to crash. It exploded on impact, killing the pilot. That put a damper on the rest of the show. That night on the base you could have heard a pin hit the floor. It seemed like when a pilot crashed, the entire base crashed. I remember going over to Betty Sue's house and listening to records with her. That night her dad came in and turned down the volume and said, "Kids, this is a sad night." I left Betty's house early that night and on my way home I ran into Danny Dougen and Bobby Fletcher. We decided to roam the base. We walked down to the service club. Usually there were some of the younger airmen in the club, but tonight there were two guys in the whole place and they were just finishing up their hamburgers and fries. We ordered three Cherry Cokes and the lady told us that she was sorry, but they were closing for the night early. Well, that ended that, so we started walking back to the houses. When we got by the base church, we looked out to the flight line and we saw that there were extra guards on the line. There must have been a guard for every plane. When we got to the AP shack we asked the guard why there was extra security. He explained to us that it was just a precaution. We asked him what he meant by that and he replied that it was "CO orders." When we got home I asked Dad what was going on. He told me that when a plane crashed like the Thunderbird, the first thing that is thought of is sabotage so that is why everything is being watched extra carefully. The three of us then went outside and sat on the curb talking for about an hour. Then Mom called me in and said I had to take a bath for church the next morning. I never did see the Thunderbirds again until 1983 when they were at Truax Field in Madison, Wisconsin.

Sunday morning Keith and Allan Scheifer met us at our house to go to church. While we walked, I noticed that the flag on the corner was at half-mast. All during the service, the minister kept referring to the pilot that was killed the day before. I remember the minister was a big guy and a captain. He wanted us to know that the young lieutenant had given his life for us while he was trying to make us happy and proud to be a part of the United States Air Force. I think it was from that day on there was nothing better to me than the Air Force, especially my dad and the 79th squadron.

After we got home from church, Mom and Dad had decided to take a run over to our Uncle Paul's house in Harlow. Charmain was two and a half years old and she kept walking around and driving us buggy. When we first arrived my brother Paul got out of the car, ran into Paul's house and completely through it out the back door into the backyard and out to the field heading down to the little creek before Mom finally caught up to him. To this day, Uncle Paul still laughs about this incident with Paul and Mom. As usual, on the way home from Uncle Paul's, Veronica got car sick and Dad had to pull over to the side of the road so that she could puke. I think she did it for attention and so she could sit in the front of the car.

During the summer of 1958, Mom and Dad took us to a lot of castles around Suffolk. Those old Romans sure could build castles. Just about every section of land had some kind of fort rows. When we would go to the beach, it was usually to Great Yarmouth. It was the only sandy beach. Felixstowe was closer, but it was all rocks. Great Yarmouth had a better amusement park, too. We never went on any of the rides though, because of the shortage of money.

When our Scout troop moved from Bentwaters to Woodbridge, it made it a lot easier to go to Scouts. The base allowed us to use one of the huts that was next to the NCO quarters. Up in the end of the barrack, there were a lot of little pines that we would take the new Scouts into and teach them how to tie knots. Our big thing was tying them to trees and seeing if they could get back to the Scout building before the meeting was over. It was fun until this one kid was tied to a tree for three hours after the troop meeting. It sure was a bone jarring experience when this kid's father and an AP showed up at your house, after you had gone to bed, and asked if you were involved in the "little prank." Needless to say, the next morning everyone in the troop was assembled at the hall with one parent present standing behind their kid. Dad went with me. Not only was our Scout Master present but also the base commander Coronel Berrit. The coronel was a good friend of my dad's since Dad was the crew chief on his plane. Dad always had a way of getting me out of deep shit. I remember Harry Krabbie said to me that if it was not for my dad, we would be done with Boy Scouts. Harry's dad was first sergeant of the mess hall so his dad also had a lot of pull with the coronel.

It was a constant game between Harry and me with the tricks we would pull on other people. Later that year, our troop played another game. We, in one night, turned in about four fire calls between the barracks where the fire boxes were. You could pull a handle and an alarm would go off in the fire station. The first call, the fire trucks came rolling up by the barracks and realized that there was not a fire. They went back to the station thinking that it was a mistake, but when the next three alarms went off, there were more AP's than fire trucks. The first place they stopped was the troop hut. The only thing that saved me, was I was working on a project in the back room with our assistant Scout Master. The three kids that did the job were taken down to the AP shack with Larry Hamlinger. Needless to say those guys got a good butt chewing and the next morning they were picking up paper from the base parking lot all the way up to the service club. We were told if we messed with them, we would be helping them pick up the trash.

I finally got my first class rank when I left England in 1959.

FOURTEEN

When school got out for the summer, I started working for Mr. Cooper delivering milk, eggs, and bread. Mike and I started many mornings without Mr. Cooper's truck by carrying the milk up the hill to the NCO quarters. We would deliver the milk to the NCO first and then the officers' quarters. Then we would head off to Bentwaters' officers' quarters.

During this summer, Mr. Cooper got himself a new truck. It was no bigger than the Ford Angler, but it was in a truck style. We used to pack gallons of milk in it. Mike did all the driving and I would get the milk and run up the sidewalks or just to the lawn in some places, and then run back to the truck before Mike could drive away. I can remember that once we went out on an egg run toward the end of the day. Being a little tired and in a hurry to get done, I dropped some of the eggs in the back of the truck. We tried to wipe them up with some rags, but they were too dirty. Mike said to check in the glove box so I did. This was my first encounter with blue and red rubbers. Mr. Cooper was making sure he had protection when he was messing around. We laughed so much that I pissed my pants.

I made a lot of money working for Mr. Cooper. I was considered the richest kid on the base. I would take my money and buy travelers checks because there was not a savings account at the base financial office. When we returned from England in 1959, I had over six hundred dollars in traveler's checks which my mom borrowed and never gave back.

Our Little League had arranged for some of us to play a game in Felixstowe for the English people. We all rode in the back of a truck with a canvas top. When we went to Felixstowe, it was sunny. We played in one of the sports centers about one block from the seaside. I don't remember the team I was playing, but it started to rain. We had the bases loaded and it was my turn to bat and I hadn't gotten that many hits this season. The first pitch that was thrown at me I drilled down the first baseline for a triple. I would have had a home run but the kid that was running in front of me was running so slow that I had to run back to third base. Everyone in the stands was cheering me on to score a run and I had to run back! I was pissed! The next batter up was thrown a high pitch that got away from the catcher and I stole home—before the kid at bat struck out.

When we were in the outfield a kid hit a ground ball to me in left. I got it with no trouble but when I went to throw it back infield, the ball went out of my hand into the bleachers on the third base side. I jumped the fence and the kid must have thought that I wasn't going to get the ball, so he just trotted around third base toward home when all of the sudden he was looking at the catcher holding the ball I had thrown. He was out which ended the game. They had to call the game at that point because of the rain. This was my best game that I ever played in Little League.

On our way home we were again in the truck with the canvas top which leaked as if there wasn't a top at all. We figured the truck was left over from the war. After we arrived at Woodbridge, we were all just as wet as the grass in the ditches.

Summer Scout camp was at Camp Mohawk again. I did not go for the first week because I wanted to make some money. But when

Troop 277 went in July, I went along. It turned out to be quite an enjoyable time. We were camping with some English Scouts and we sure learned how to camp "roughing it" like the English Scouts did. I think that I learned more that one week than I did in my other five years of scouting.

We again went camping at the Haunted Church. Man, did those British Scouts get us! We would go out for training and when we would get back, our tents would be tied up with our bed rolls in the trees. We set traps and then we went running after them. We traded tricks with them since we were in out tents and they were in theirs. We had a good chance to get them. We had the old-style pup tent the Army used since 1911 and the English Scouts had big safari tents. When we collapsed theirs, it took them a while to get out of it. Fortunately, no one got hurt and when the week was over we all traded patches and addresses, shook hands and went our separate ways. I never did earn another patch that week at camp, but almost got first class. My biggest problem was morris code. These days if you ask a Scout about morris code, he'll ask you what in the hell you are talking about.

During the summer of 1958, we made a few trips to Felixstowe. Dad would put five gallons of gas in the old Angler and off to the coast we would go. We usually would walk the beach front and buy ice cream sandwiches made from the best ice cream I've ever had. We would always go out to the harbor and watch people ride the little ferry over to the other side of the harbor. We would get a good laugh when the waves would come up over the bow of the little motor boat.

About tea time, which is around 5:00 p.m., we would begin the drive back to the base and pass along all the sites of war. To this day, I can still see the grass runways where the Spitfires took off for the Battle of Britain.

The 79th went TDY to Morocco again and during this time, we kids sure drove the AP nuts. I remember the new sergeant major of the AP was big into fancy drills and nice, neat uniforms. We kids used to mess with their drill until one kid got carried off by two AP's and put into the base stockade until his mother showed up.

Fall of 1958 came and we got ready for school once again. It was a bad fall because I knew it would be our last in England. I was starting seventh grade junior high at the time.

For the first time I had three teachers. Mr. Brenett was my homeroom teacher. He was a navy academy graduate and a very big guy. He was the only teacher to give me a spanking. One day, I was fooling around in music class with John Livington. After class Mr. Brenett gave us a choice, give up recess or take three swats. John Livington was bigger than I, so his hits didn't hurt him quite as much as mine.

Mr. Brickner was our English teacher. He was from Sheboygan, Wisconsin. He used to talk to us about his play acting in Wisconsin. He was one of the older teachers in the school but he was loved by all of us even though he had a hell of a temper.

Mr. Baily on the other hand was a very quiet guy. The only noise he made was when he was sucking on his spearmint lifesavers. He taught social studies. We learned a lot in his class because of the fact that if anyone went to sleep he had a little stick that he would smack on your desk. After you woke up, he would bite down on his lifesaver, give you a half smile, then turn around and walk away.

Our junior high also had a woman teacher. I didn't have her and for this I was glad. I remember one of my friends told us after school that this kid, whose name I will not tell, had jacked off in class and when he had his orgasm he started to yell. Ms. Jones ran over asking him what was the matter and he told her that it was nothing—that he just had a muscle cramp. Everyone in the class laughed because they knew what he did. This boy was the fastest guy on our football team. However, he only got to play a few games because he was ineligible due to poor grades. The one game that I do remember was when this boy was playing against Wethersfield. I was playing end and was supposed to block the end in, but before I hit the guy I was going for, this boy was around me and halfway down the field to score a touchdown. We won that game. It was always a joy to beat Wethersfield since they were the home squadron of the 79th.

Football season ended with our last game at Lakenheath. I remember that field was the roughest I played on in all my days of football. It was located on the end of the runway. The base football team of Woodbridge was doing really well in 1958. They were kicking everybody all over the isle of England. It was something to be standing on the sideline when the 79th would take the field. During halftime, they would have the third Air Force band play. During one game the base arranged to have the Highland Scotches band with their bagpipes and they all played. That was the best pipe music I have ever heard.

During one game, they had a bunch of beautiful girls (I don't know where they came from) come play in a halftime performance. I don't remember ever seeing any cheerleaders on the sidelines for any of the games, but during this one in particular, we kids sure had fun passing out bottles of water and towels to the team during timeouts!

I remember that during another game it was raining so hard you couldn't see the end zone. We had a quarterback who could throw half the distance of the field. In this game, he was throwing it and nobody was there to catch it. We won that game 6-0. We scored with a quarterback sneak on the second yard line late in the fourth quarter. The field never did get green after that game.

The 79th wound up beating everyone with the exception of Brizenorton. With Brizenorton being the headquarters in England, they got the pick of the men in the Air Force. We got a few good guys. I remember a guy who was a dog pilot and he was a good running back. He could fly the F100 with hands down and that attitude carried over onto the football field.

FIFTEEN

My paper route began to grow a little. The officer was having new houses put into operation. I started out delivering twenty-three papers everyday, and when we left in 1959, I was up to sixty-eight. I would have had seventy, but one set of quarters burned down.

I remember riding out to the flight lines in the mornings and being told to go home because the plane was fogged in.

Our Scout troop went to Lakenheath for a Scout campout. It had to be the first camp outing that we went on that it did not rain. The excitement of the camp was when a bunch of guys went out and knocked down a bunch of tents from other troops. Some of us guys were standing around and all of a sudden somebody shouted, "Fire in tent!" When the word went out some of us ran over with Larry Hamerlinger and collapsed the tent. By this time the fire truck had arrived and was spraying down the tent. Later, the AP squadron put on a show with their attack dog. That let us guys know that we sure did not want to go into the restricted area. Our troop came home with a few ribbons. One thing, Larry Hamlinger and Bob Schwartz taught was how to survive under pressure.

Not to be outdone, the Wethersfield base CO invited the 3rd Air Force Boy Scout troops to his base for a weekend campout. Wethersfield had one of the wettest fields I have ever seen. To make things worse, it rained most of the weekend. On Friday night, when we pitched our tents, we slept with our heads on the chow boxers. Some of us older Scouts used gear boxes and even Bob Schwarz. The highlight for our troop was when Harry Hamlinger pitched a parachute tent, and we got to use it as the main tent since it was raining so hard. We even cooked and ate in it. When Harry cooked Saturday night's meal, it consisted of hamburgers straight out of the crate. The manufacture had put plenty of salt on them, but Harry thought they could use some more. Well, he did add more and nobody could eat them. When we threw the hamburgers out of the tent into the junk hole, which was full of water, the water bubbled up like a volcano.

The rain did not let up, so later Saturday afternoon, the Wetherfield CO called us all together and passed out a few awards. Our troop got one for being able to adapt to conditions. Also, we got the prize for being the most supplied for salty hamburgers. We let Harry go up and get the award, and on his way back from getting the ribbon, he tripped in the mud and fell right on his face. Everyone laughed and this pissed him off, so he started throwing mud at some Scouts from the other troops, which in turn would have triggered a mud fight if the CO hadn't broke it up.

We loaded on the bus with all our wet gear and headed home. I remember Larry Hamlinger took off his Air Force boots and began scraping off the mud that was about an inch thick on the bottom of them. All the way home, it rained and our bus was cold and damp due to our gear being on board. When we finally got back to the base, we unloaded the bus and hung our gear in the Scout hall. I remember coming in the front door and Mom hollered, "What happened to you!?!" I was wet and covered in mud from head to foot from hanging up the gear. My sleeping bag never did loose the mud stains on it.

Basketball season started for 1958 and I was one of eleven guys that tried out for the team. They suited up eleven guys for the games. I got to play some, but I had a problem with dribbling and running at the same time. Bentwaters' gym was a big drafty building. I think it was an old equipment building with a hard wood floor put in it. We had such a good record that I don't remember it too well.

During the middle of the season, I got sick and couldn't play. I was the second guy to get sick. One of our guards, by the name of Mike, got Rheumatic fever and was out most of the season. At the end of the season, the third Air Force base had a tournament for all the schools and would only allow ten guys on the team so we had tryouts and I got cut. What pissed me off was that there was a new kid on the base that came and tried out for the team. Mr. Brunett was our coach and he told me that if they won any medals that I could have his. Anyway, I took my bag to school the day the team was due to ship out and went to talk to Ms. Gardner and told her how I had been cheated out of going with the team. Ms. Gardner talked to Mr. Brunett and I guess chewed his ass because he came and got me out of music class and took me out into the hall to chew me out. I went into the bathroom crying and while I was there, my friend Mose Jackson came in and tried to comfort me. While we were in the bathroom, a little dog came in and tried to screw Mose's leg. He yelled at the dog and the next thing we knew, Mr. Brickner was in the bathroom yelling at us for disturbing his class. Poor Mose, his black face became white. We recovered, and Mose and I went back to class still pissed off and still not going with the team. Mr. Brunett came around and got the basketball team and loaded them on the bus for Scholthorp. Our team did not do very well and some of the boys had a problem in the dorm while they were at Scholthorp. It made me feel really good when one of them turned out to be the new kid that beat me out of the slot for the team.

Christmas of 1958 was our last Christmas in England. Mom invited her brothers, Adrian and Graham, to spend some time with us. I remember the one gift I got was a rug that Mom and I made and I still have to this day in our bedroom. Grandma came and stayed a few days with us after Christmas. At that time I did not know Grandma and Ralph (he was Grandma's second husband) were having a rough time at home. Within a year, they were divorced.

Every Friday night during school that year, some of the girls in our class would have dances at their houses. Most of the girls would dance together while us guys would just sit there and watch. One night, Mike Steel fell in love with my girl and it lasted that night and Saturday morning until I talked her into coming back to me. She was pissed off that I didn't dance with her, and Mike was willing to dance all night if his parents would let him.

I kept bringing in money working every morning delivering papers in the office quarters and from delivering milk, eggs and bread on Saturdays. By the time I left Woodbridge in June of 1959, I had made over six hundred dollars in travelers checks When we returned from England in 1959, I had over six hundred dollars in traveler's checks which my mom borrowed and never gave back.

Mr. Cooper taught me how to get up early and he taught me how to work twelve hours a day. Delivering milk was just like the mail. Rain, snow or hail never stopped us from delivering milk, bread or eggs.

SIXTEEN

1959

On Sunday nights during the winter, we used to go to the church and have good times raising hell. We would watch the movies, eat the donuts, and then go out and ring door bells and try to run away before we got caught. There were four of us guys that ran together and looked after my little brother, Paul.

The last Easter at Woodbridge, Paul was in this Easter egg hunt and Danny and Harry helped pick up eggs. We said we were trying to win our age bracket but just before they counted the eggs the three of us put our eggs in Paul's basket. When the minister counted Paul's eggs, he had twelve more than the nearest kid to him so they gave Paul a five pound chocolate Easter bunny. It was so big that Danny carried it while I carried Paul on my shoulders. Mom and Dad couldn't figure out how Paul had found so many eggs until we told them. Mom got mad, but Dad just laughed.

The weekend after Easter, our troop went out for a campout. It was out on the heather behind the base at Woodbridge. We took a bunch of tender-foot Scouts out so they could pass cooking. This was the first time I saw butterscotch pudding burned. The good thing was that we older Scouts had Harry put together some C-rations for us to eat. I kept saying all the way back to the base that those kids would have the shits. The next morning, Harry and I kept looking for the kids that had tried to kill us with their cooking but they never made it. They were too sick to make it to school.

May 1, 1959, is a day that I will always remember as being the most scared. Our Scout troop went to London to visit the Scout troop we had gotten to know at camp. The morning started all screwed up. Some airmen had gotten on our bus thinking we were going to a horse race. When we got to Chlemford, they ended up getting off and taking the train back to the racetrack. Being that it was May Day, it was a big day in racing. Even the Queen of England's horse ran in the race. Anyway, after we had let the airmen out of the bus and we were on our way to London, we stopped at one of the bases to eat lunch. After lunch, we made a few wrong turns and wound up on Trafalgar Square. There was one thing wrong with us being there. It was May Day, the day which communists protest and hold their demonstration. They really went bananas. We just happened to be in a big blue bus that said "United States Air Force" down the side. The communists were throwing rocks at the bus and were beginning to surround it and shake it while trying not to tip it over. Our bus driver told Larry Hamlinger (our Scout Master) to have us kids lay down and not look out the windows. It's hard to believe that we got out of there, but we did, and as we rounded the corner to continue on our way, we stood up and flipped off the communists. Larry was pissed off at all of us.

After finally getting to our destination, we had stopped on a big hill so that we could look down on London. After ten minutes, I was in a fight with somebody. Although I do not remember his name, I do remember seeing his lip splitting out after one punch (and yes, I caught hell for that, too).

We arrived at the big hall and found that the English Scouts were having a party for us. We stayed there until about 8:00 p.m. and got out of London without any more excitement.

My final Scout outing with troop 277 came when our troop went to Camp Gillwill. Gillwill is the camp of Lord Badown Powell, the founder of Boy Scouts. As usual, our bus got lost and almost ran out of gas. Our driver had gone over Friday night and got gas at another base while our green bar patrol went to Gillwill and pitched our tents. We discovered that one of our Scouts had brought along a canister of whiskey. We formed a belt line in the woods so the English Scouts did not see us. After we beat up the kid, we went back to Scout business.

On Saturday, we competed with the English Scouts in different categories. We discovered we were not as good as we thought. On Saturday night, there was a big camp fire with all the English Scouts and the two American troops. The highlight was when Mrs. Badon Powell and her son came out in front of us all. The master of ceremony introduced each troop. It was quite an honor being able to salute Mrs. Powell and her son. After the campfire, we traded badges with the English Scouts. Some of them were from New Zealand and Australia. This was a camparee for the British commonwealth.

On Sunday morning we got up, ate breakfast, took down our tents, and started to get ready to go home. We got all packed up and got on the bus while the driver and Larry were checking out the map. All of the sudden, a kid hollered "Go home you damn Yanks!" We all bailed out of the bus quicker than if it were on fire. We beat up on some of the English Scouts and they beat up on some of us before the Scout Masters broke it up. As we pulled out of Gillwill, we saluted the camp and Scouts of the English commonwealth. We let them know that we were not all that bad even though we had just kicked their ass. The camp patch we got was a wood badge patch which is still used today.

After Scouts, Mr. Cooper kept me busy right up to the time that we left. I remember trying to teach this kid my paper route. I often wondered on foggy days if he got lost down on the flight line just waiting for the Stars and Stripes.

We went to see Uncle Clive and his family. Grandma Dawson had split with Ralph. I remember Uncle Robin had taken his motor bike apart and it was sitting in pieces in Uncle Clive's garage. It was during this trip that my cousin Chris and I started a fire that burned something in or by his garage. I never remembered this until Uncle Paul told me about it in January 1990.

Uncle Robin was in the reserves so he went off on duty. I remember teasing him and he threatened to throw me in the sea. Uncle Clive had a fish pond in his backyard. We tried to push Veronica in the pond and Mom came out to kick my ass.

Dad, Clive, Chris, Paul and I went out to the old fort at the break water. I remember standing by the water with it spraying in our faces and Paul almost falling in. There were ships coming and going in the harbor. The ships I saw in 1985 were about twice the size as the ships that day, though. The fort is falling apart more now, but it still has the gun placement and track for transport carts.

We did not stay in Loftus that year, but we went to see the lady, Mrs. Dawson, from my birth place in Easington. Then, we went up to Sheffield to visit Grandma and Adrian. They were living in a little trailer. I don't remember why they were there, but I do remember that it was parked next to a construction site. As we drove in and out of it, we saw the big Sheffield steel factories. Back in the 1950's, Sheffield was a knife manufacturing town.

Our school had a fun night. It was a fundraising program and I was assigned to the basketball court. The only customer I had was my Mom. I think she shot four times at the basket and only missed once.

The school had the athletic banquet for the football and basketball team. I got my first and only letter. I rode to the banquet with another family. Dad was TDY to another base and Mom did not go with me.

Mr. Berrett was giving out the letters for football and when he called me up for my letter he said, "Here is the guy that was supposed to block for our running back, but by the time he got off the line, Bobby had got around Mike and scored a touch down for us." I did not get to play in the basketball tournament so I did not get a letter.

In April, some of us guys went riding in the Suffolk Heath. I remember riding out to Bordsey and looking at the big radar screens. We were standing there and all of a sudden a hawker hunter came flying at tree top level. I thought that it may have been a German fighter during the war, or even worse, a Russian mig. We then rode our bikes to a small store and bought a pop and a bag of potato chips. We made a round and wound up by the ferry that went to old Felexstow. I never did cross it, but I often wanted to. It was a small, single-engine, ten passenger.

In May, we had a school picnic out in a park that was near a sandy beach. I remember sitting there with Gerdous Berrit and talking with her and planning to stay in contact after I went back to the States, but it never happened. Harry Krabby stood around telling jokes and teasing the girls. We all played a game of softball. When we got ready to go back to school, Harry Alaxandria had to take a piss so he went into the woods. In front of the trees there were tank blocks. He jumped out of the wood and up on top of the blocks and acted like Tarzan. This was the last school function at Bentwaters.

The following week was the last week of school. Mom and Dad had everything packed up on the last day we were at Woodbridge and shipped it all back to the States. My classic comic book that Veronica had loaned to the Kotch girls was not brought back until after the packers had left our house. Half of the comic book was torn up. I was so pissed off, but that was Veronica's usual way of "if it wasn't hers it was going to be destroyed."

The day before we left, Mom sent me to Ipswich to get her money out from the co-op. I was wearing some old, grubby clothes and was mistakenly thought to be an escapee from the reformatory at Bordsay by a big English cop as I was passing over the bridge. I showed him my military department ID card and told him the reason for my ripped clothes. I got to Ipswich, did Mom's errand and got back to the base without any other holdups.

I didn't know that Dennis Green and some of the other kids had planned a surprise going away party for me. They gave me a cigarette lighter with a map of England on it. I forgot the gal's name, but she gave me a kiss and started to cry. I kept Dennis Green's address and wrote him a letter one year later. I have not heard from him since.

That last night was pretty spooky around the house. Paul was playing with his little friends on the floor, Dad was lying on the couch, and Mom was crying in the kitchen. Gosh, Mom had looked after the house that we had lived in for over two years.

The next day, June 11, 1959, was ship out day for us. Late in the afternoon, a van came and picked us up to take us to Lakenheath for our plane back to the States. When we arrived at Lakenheath, Dad noticed they had the engine covers off and a guy was standing on the wing, defueling the plane we were supposed to board. While we were waiting, a staff car pulled up and out stepped a captain. It was Dr. Fetgerld who had done the operation on my foot in 1957.

It was around 11:00 p.m. when they finally got us airborne. I was sitting in the seat next to Dad and looked over at Mom. She was crying because she knew this would be her last time in England. (Mom died in 1970 and Dad died in 1984). We landed in Prestwick, Scotland for refueling, and they wound up having to work on the plane. We finally took off from Scotland and about halfway over the ocean the 'No Smoking' and 'Fasten Your Seatbelt' light came on and the plane began to shake. Paul thought that the pilot had done this for him because, just before, he had stopped and talked to him. About half an hour later, we were told to put on our life vests and then they had Dad get up and join the rest of the crew in the cockpit. We finally landed in Gander, Newfoundland. They worked on the plane for about two hours. I remember that we were on the ground long enough to go into the mess hall and get something to eat, although I do not remember what we ate at Gander except for waffles and hot applesauce. We took off from Gander and they said that the plane was fixed. Well, it was… until we hit a thunderstorm over Maine. It stayed with us until we got to McGuire Air Force base in New Jersey where the Byrd family re-entered the United States after four years of great times in England.

This poem was written in early 1943 by Mr. Melvin Beebe. Mr. Beebe was the foster father of my dad, his sister, and brother. In 1943, Dad was on the B17 Bombers flying out of Thurleigh, England. Mr. Beebe owned and operated a big dairy farm in the county of Winnebago, just south of Oshkosh, Wisconsin. In 1959, it was the first place we stopped in Wisconsin when we got back from England. The poem here doesn't have anything to do with my book, but it was in Dad's Air Force papers that go back to WWII. I want to thank my friend, Mose Jackson, of Lancaster, California for convincing me to put this in my book.

<u>An Airman's Prayer</u>

Almighty God who

Rules the skies

From darkest night

To glad sunrise

Guide us safe

Thru thy vast vault;

From which the stars

May not revolt

We do not seek

To plunder, prey

In this mad fray.

We gladly see

A world at peace,

From war and strife

We ask surcease.

Heed our prayer

From thy high throne

Thou, Lord can grant,

And thou alone.